Thomas Fleiner is a constitutional specialist, with a practical bent. He has a broad familiarity with constitutions and systems of government throughout the world, drawn from both scholarship and practical experience. Based in Switzerland, he is Director of the Institute of Federalism, at the University of Fribourg. His particular interests include governance in ethnically divided societies, human rights and federalism. He has studied and taught in Switzerland, the United States, France, Yugoslavia, Germany, Belgium and Israel, and has been a member of the International Committee of the Red Cross. His services as a consultant on aspects of constitutional design have been sought in Africa, the wider Europe, Asia and South America. From 1995-99, he was President of the International Association of Constitutional Law.

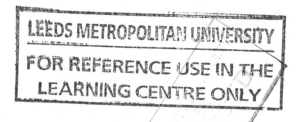

What are
Human Rights?

What are Human Rights?

Thomas Fleiner

Translated from the German by
Nicholas Anson
Centre for Comparative Constitutional Studies
University of Melbourne

The Federation Press
1999

Published in Sydney by

The Federation Press
71 John St, Leichhardt, NSW, 2040
PO Box 45, Annandale, NSW, 2038
Ph: (02) 9552 2200 Fax: (02) 9552 1681
E-mail: info@fedpress.aust.com
Website: http://www.fedpress.aust.com

National Library of Australia Cataloguing-in-Publication data:

Fleiner-Gerster, Thomas
[Was sind menschenrechle. English]
What are human rights?

ISBN 1 86287 328 3 ✓

1.   Human rights. I. Anson, Nicholas. II. Title.

323

Typeset by The Federation Press, Leichhardt, NSW.
        Printed by Southwood Press Pty Ltd, Marrickville , NSW.

Translator's Note

In *What are Human Rights?*, Thomas Fleiner employs a conversational style which for the most part is precise and occasionally poetic, indeed reminiscent of the Universal Declaration of Human Rights itself. I conceived my task as translator to adhere faithfully to what he says and to maintain to the best of my ability the atmosphere he creates. I have therefore generally avoided all paraphrasing not otherwise required by language differences and the need to preserve the conversational style. Occasionally I have added an explanatory word or two, and broken sentences of typically German length into sizes more appealing to the English reader.

Like many translators, I have struggled with the appropriate translation of Nietzsche's *Übermensch*. While some translators leave the term untranslated, others have used Superman or Overman. All three of these options strike me as unsatisfactory. In the end, I have decided to use "superior human being". This is intended to avoid connotations of superheros, and preserve the idea of a hierarchy within the human race. The inverted commas are intended to signal that the author does not support the hierarchy which the term *Übermensch* implies.

Beside the usual difficulties of translation, there are challenges stemming from the fact that *What are Human Rights?* deals with two different legal systems. While the differences between the common-law tradition of countries such as the United Kingdom and the United States and the civil law systems of the European continent should not be overstated, differences do remain which lead to translation problems. The central term *Rechtsstaat* is itself an example of this. When contrasted with the English equivalent, "rule of law", *Rechtsstaat* – which literally means "law-state" – reveals the greater emphasis that the German legal tradition places on the state. Depending on the context, I translate *Rechtsstaat* either as "rule of law" or "constitutional democracy".

Continental justifications for human rights, particularly when drawn from the Kantian tradition of natural law, will not be familiar to many readers in the English-speaking world. I have chosen to capitalise "Reason", for example, when describing human beings as endowed with Reason (*vernunftbegabt*), so that it is clear that Fleiner is invoking a concept embedded in a rich intellectual tradition.

The translation of the various types of rights can also pose occasional difficulties stemming from differences between civil and common-law traditions. *Grundrechte* include "basic" or "fundamental rights" protected by the Constitution, and so may also be translated as "constitutional rights". The catalogue of human rights discussed by Fleiner is wider than that typically in issue in the common-law world, yet a "right to linguistic freedom" is clearly of increasing importance in multi-ethnic states such as the United States, Canada, Britain and Australia.

In many cases, the German is both rich and fluid enough to make a rigid adherence to one-to-one correlations neither possible nor desirable. This is the case, for example, for the broad range of German words having to do with power and authority, bureaucracy and administration. In such cases, the demands of context and readability are decisive, particularly given Fleiner's conversational writing-style.

In order to avoid sexist language, I have (with the author's assent) alternated the use of feminine and masculine pronouns where appropriate, and capitalised "Man" and "Mankind" where they are used without reference to the male sex. It is nevertheless unavoidable that the gender-specific nature of German articles and pronouns leave an imprint on the English translation.

Nicholas Anson

Contents

Contents

Preface to the English edition

At the end of the 20th century, the concept of human rights is widely accepted. The Universal Declaration of Human Rights has been in existence for 50 years. Most people in most countries agree that human rights deserve protection and respect.

Beyond this level of general agreement, however, human rights are often disputed and easily misunderstood. Some of the main questions raised are these:

- What kind of rights deserve to be described as human rights, attracting greater protection and respect? The main division here is between civil and political rights on the one hand and social, economic and cultural rights on the other. As a generalisation, developed Western liberal democracies believe the former should have constitutional protection or, at least, be given some special status through the system of law. Developing democracies in countries with socialist systems of law, on the other hand, accord higher priority to social and economic rights.

- Which particular rights, in each of these categories, are human rights? Sometimes the answer is obvious, because the rights have been acknowledged for so long. Others have been recognised more recently, however. The right to privacy is an example. The right to a healthy environment is another. The extent to which genetic experimentation is permissible or infringes human rights is a contemporary question for our times.

- If resources are limited, which rights have priority, if it is necessary to choose? And if one person's right is in conflict with another's, how should that be resolved?

- How are human rights best protected? Through the design of a system of government? Through courts? What role can the international community properly play, in human rights protection?

- What is the relationship between human rights and democracy? Are human rights integral to democracy or a qualification of it? How can the interests of individuals or minority groups be balanced against the needs of a community as a whole?

- What does self-determination mean? How can it be achieved without breaking up the state?

The central purpose of this book is to explain human rights, canvassing these and a host of other questions. Its intended audience is people without technical knowledge of the law or highly developed theoretical understanding, although specialists will enjoy it as well. The book will be of interest to anyone who would like to be challenged to think about what human rights mean and how they can be given practical effect. The text is a pleasure to read, because it is so clearly written. At the same time, it engages the reader actively through practical examples and thought-provoking anecdotes, drawn from a variety of legal traditions. Fifty years after the Universal Declaration of Human Rights committed the world, to "their universal and effective recognition and observance", this is a timely contribution to world debate not only about the past but about the future.

The author, Thomas Fleiner, is a Swiss. The book is grounded in his deep understanding of the European legal tradition, of the sensitivities which Swiss experience suggest are necessary for making a multi-cultural nation work, of the practical issues thrown up daily by human rights in a sophisticated democracy like Switzerland. But both the text and its relevance range well beyond the Swiss republic. Thomas Fleiner has lived and worked in common law as well as continental jurisdictions. He has practical understanding of the operation of government in countries as diverse as South Africa, Russia, the United States, China and Columbia. From time to time, he has been called upon to advise on conflicts raising human rights questions in the most acute form; most notably, in former Yugoslavia. His wide-ranging practical knowledge of governance in most major regions of the world add immeasurably to both the interest and usefulness of the book.

It is a measure of this usefulness that the book has been published already in German, French and Spanish and will appear soon in Chinese as well. It has been a pleasure to be associated with the English version, on several grounds. The Centre for Comparative Constitutional Studies, University of Melbourne, has a brief to make constitutional issues, broadly conceived, accessible to the general public – which is exactly what *What are Human Rights?* does. It is satisfying to be able to contribute to a task which has demonstrable practical benefits for many people. It has been an interesting intellectual exercise, from the standpoint of comparative constitutional law, to reflect on the requirements of translating a work grounded in a particular legal tradition for easy comprehension by an audience grounded in another. And finally, it is a pleasure because Thomas Fleiner is a long-standing friend.

The translation is the work of Nicholas Anson. He approached the task with meticulous care, informed by his own interest in different political philosophical traditions. He has my admiration for the final result and it has been a lot of fun to work together. But the principle achievement, of course, is that of Thomas Fleiner himself, who has drawn on his prodigious stores of energy and commitment to make a lasting contribution to the human rights debate.

Cheryl Saunders
Centre for Comparative Constitutional Studies
University of Melbourne
July 1999

Preface to the German edition

Barely a day passes without reference to human rights in the media. Yet few know exactly what this means. The aim of this book is to make the complex subject of human rights more understandable and to make readers familiar with it by way of concrete examples. Different human rights issues will be introduced through such examples, rather than by systematic and comprehensive analysis.

Professor Lidija Basta read through the manuscript and made many suggestions most of which I have been able to take into account. Thank you. She has had both academic and painful personal experience with the problems of human and minority rights in the former and existing Yugoslavia. This, together with her empathy and sound philosophical understanding of the questions of legitimacy and the position of minorities, have helped me a lot. In particular, they have improved my understanding of the difficult and complex relationship between the problems of human rights on the one hand and those of the protection of minorities on the other.

I would also like to thank my assistant Anton Greber for his valued suggestions and critical reflections on the manuscript. His suggestions particularly enriched the different examples used. My daughter Daniela deserves special thanks for checking whether the manuscript is suitable for school-leavers.

For proof-reading and editing I am indebted to my assistant, Jeanne-Dominique Prodolliet.

It only remains to express my hope that this book will improve the understanding and interest of readers in human rights issues. If, having read this account, one reader or another is prompted actively to support the protection of human rights, the book will have achieved more than I dare to hope.

Thomas Fleiner

1

From Human Dignity

It is a beautiful summer's morning on a beach. I have made a free and independent decision to write rather than to bathe, to drink coffee or to turn on the television. What has this got to do with human dignity? A great deal: unlike all other forms of life, human beings set the course of their own actions, at least in part.

Humans can establish priorities and be guided by particular value judgments. Value judgments and priorities are determined partly by needs and partly by rational considerations. Through their capacity to reason, humans can choose the values which guide their actions and determine what is good and bad for them. Humans also can prepare for the future. They alone have the ability to choose between two possible courses of action, and to decide in favour of the one that appears to be the most rational, the most interesting, the most risky or the most convenient.

Only human beings have enough inherent freedom to recognise which decision is correct and the opportunity to act accordingly. Anyone who intrudes on someone's inherent freedom violates that person's inherent dignity. Consequently, those who speak of human dignity must respect the freedom which humans need in order to form their own opinions and to act on them. Furthermore, they must give each person the opportunity to develop according to his or her own plan for the future. Every form of coercion which significantly restricts a person's freedom of choice is an attack on human dignity. Freedom of choice is an essential element of the inner core of humanity.

However, a person's dignity also extends to everything that shaped that person: surroundings, family, history, culture and language, collectively described as a person's identity, a person's roots. Anyone who robs a person of the framework of reference which determines her judgment and action, impinges on her dignity just as much as if they had forced her to do an act which she would never freely undertake. Those who refuse to recognise a person's historical, linguistic and cultural identity damage the roots of her existence that are part of her inherent dignity.

Human beings are not just free; they are also each unique and need to be respected in their uniqueness. Consequently, someone is hurt to the core if he is ridiculed because of his race, nationality or religion. Human dignity demands that a person's uniqueness, his individuality, is respected and that he is not rejected as part of a despised race. If someone cannot develop personally as an individual, then an attack has been made on the inherent core of his humanity and personhood.

However, we must not go to the other extreme and view human beings in isolation from other people or even from society. They are not like that at all. Indeed, when I write this book I assume that there are people who can read it. It needs publishers and bookshops. My computer needs electricity. I myself have enjoyed a particular education. In his individuality Man is no isolated atom in society. Rather, every person lives with others. A person's freedom is largely determined by the surroundings in which she lives and which mould her. A person's dignity will take a different form depending on the society's level of development and her cultural or religious surroundings.

But the most inner part of a person, the core of his identity, which allows him, if necessary, to break out of society, which enables him to act as a loner, which gives a person like Salman Rushdie the strength to write a book that is critical of the religion to which he belongs: this inherent core is inviolable. It belongs to the most elementary part of individual human dignity.

Attacks on human dignity are not just restricted to subtle and sophisticated techniques, such as truth drugs, public disparagement, ridicule of particular races, or social discrimination against particular nationalities, races or religious communities. When people no longer have control over their own bodies, when they are humiliatingly dehumanised and beaten until they are mental and physical cripples, their human dignity has been scarred and damaged to a point where redress is impossible. Physical integrity is the last place where a person can be himself. If it is destroyed, then there is no room left to be human.

2

Human Rights as a Plaything of Politics

Representatives of governments who travel to China call for human rights to be observed. In Cambodia, people call for human rights to be respected and monitored by international organisations. South Africa has adopted a new constitution which is supposed to guarantee human rights and equal opportunity for all inhabitants regardless of race or religion. In some African countries the rights of people are abused and flagrantly violated through ethnic conflict, military government and police terror. In France citizens of North African origin protest against serious discrimination; in Germany politicians call on the police to provide better protection of foreigners; and in Switzerland political asylum-seekers and refugees are exposed to the massive pressure of forces that are hostile to foreigners.

Human rights have become the plaything of politics. The Council of Europe condemns Turkey for breaching human rights in its handling of the Kurdish question. Turkey in turn accuses the Western states of Europe of taking advantage of the politics of human rights in order to undermine the Turkish state, indeed to subvert and destroy it through their support for the Kurds.

Islamic fundamentalists dismiss human rights as a monstrous product of the Enlightenment's Christian origin. For them, human rights have no validity in a state that is committed to religious goals. For a state must give effect to the word of God as holy commandment, and persecute those who flout it. Those who break the law of God cannot invoke human rights. There can be no right to religious freedom in these states; for you cannot invoke a right to make mistakes.

International conferences are convened to improve the protection of human rights. The Organisation for Security and Cooperation in Europe runs a government conference every year to examine how human rights might better be realised in participating countries. The United Nations demands annual reports about the observance of human rights from its various member-states. More than 40 years ago Europe introduced its own convention for the protection of human rights, the European Convention for the Protection of Human Rights and Fundamental Freedoms. This convention allows citizens of countries which are parties to it to take their own countries to the European Court of Human Rights.

The United States has an ambivalent relationship with human rights. While it criticises the human rights record of other countries, dozens of sentenced murderers await implementation of the death penalty, which could come immediately or at some time in an uncertain future. The European Court of Human Rights regards the constant and drawn out fear of death as severe torture.

In the Balkans, policies of protecting human and minority rights are used to support members of one's own ethnic group in a neighbouring state in their opposition to the politics of that government. In Baltic countries, Russian minorities are forced to make up for the sins of the Soviet Union in its oppression of the Baltic republics over the past 60 years.

Human rights are rejected by the Chinese as instruments designed to destroy communist rule.

Many who, in the name of the "right to life", want to outlaw the termination of pregnancies, support the reintroduction of the death-penalty. Conversely, advocates of peace in the interests of preserving life are quick to call for liberal abortion laws.

Human rights have become central to the consciousness of today's society. They have become important political instruments for the denunciation of governments, states and parties. Human rights are a central preoccupation of a media which wants to alarm the public.

But you are entitled to ask yourself whether these activities in the end will *really* benefit those who are already affected or who potentially are endangered by human rights abuses. In many cases politicians are concerned with their popularity at home, rather than with the victims. Policies of protecting human rights help their electoral fortunes, but not the real people who are affected. This discredits human rights. They must not be abused for political purposes.

The politicisation of human rights tempts politicians to brag about how well human rights are protected in their own country, even where this is imaginary, while vigorously condemning the human rights abuses of other countries. Yet anyone who is blind to human rights abuses in his own country is a poor judge of others.

So policies of improving human rights are often misused to discredit opposing governments, to support political demands for the autonomy of minorities and to demonise whole states and nations. Political protagonists only very rarely are concerned primarily with helping the victims of human rights abuses. Help requires patience, discretion, staying power, political subtlety and, most importantly, unselfish human commitment.

3

What is a Human Right?

A family of refugees from Turkey has just received notification that their application for asylum has been rejected. Now the family is faced with deportation to Turkey. The father fears that he will be thrown into jail on arrival and tortured. The mother does not know how she can cope there with her three children. The family has already been living in Switzerland for years. The oldest child is in grade four and speaks Swiss-German better than the language of her parents. She has school friends with whom she plays after finishing her homework.

The uncertainty, the dependence on the Swiss authorities, the fear of further persecution, the teasing of other children, the reproachful expression of the teacher, the understanding sympathy of the employer, the well-meaning words of fellow workers and the missionary enthusiasm of some representatives of aid agencies that look after the family – all these are a burden on a family that lives in a small flat, trying to raise children, look after the adults and maintain a healthy family life.

If the family had an ordinary life the mother and father would have normal jobs; they would be valued by their colleagues, and they could offer to help friends and other people. People would listen to them, ask them for advice and seek their favour. The children could visit other families to play with their children; they could show-off their new presents and be proud of their parents. They would not be left out of things by their teacher or ostracised by students for being "annoying" members of the class. They would not have to live with open or hidden accusations that they lower the class average by holding up the others, making it impossible for many of their fellow students to pass the entrance exam at prestigious secondary schools.

The most elementary human right is the right of each individual to stay in the surroundings in which she finds herself, to live like all the others, to develop, to live, to work, to relax, to find out things for herself, to be with other people, to marry and raise children: *human rights are the rights of human beings to live according to their nature and with other human beings.*

Naturally, people's opportunities vary greatly according to their aptitudes and inclinations, according to their needs and wishes. People are to a greater or lesser extent free, depending on their social surroundings, their stage of technical and economical development and political circumstances. If people are allowed to enjoy their freedom, they will develop differently.

However, when they can no longer develop naturally, because, for example, they disagree with the politics of the government or are not entitled to the civil rights of the state in which they live, because they belong to a different religious community or even because they do not have the "right" skin colour or sex, then their most elementary human rights have been violated. The state must not restrict people's development, must not simply throw them in jail just because they have a different skin colour, or do not declare their support for the official religion, are female or belong to the political opposition.

Human rights do not mean that a resident of Indonesia has to have access to the same freeways and universities as a resident of Canada. But the residents of Canada, like those of Indonesia, must have the same opportunities to develop their natural abilities within their country as everyone else in that country. The police may not order them from their apartments, merely because they do not have the "right" skin colour or nationality; the government may not throw them in prison, just because they do not agree with the prevailing politics; the school-principal may not bar them from craft classes, just because they are girls.

The state must not force people to do things just because they do not have a desired characteristic. Skin colour, sex and cultural, emotional and family roots belong to the identity of a person. If you disadvantage people because of their background, they will feel profoundly belittled. Everyone is rightly proud of his identity and his roots. They are a part of every person. If you disadvantage someone on account of these, you spare his body, only to damage or destroy his soul.

Admittedly we are all bound by social forces. We cannot afford every type of car. Have our human rights therefore been violated? Not at all: human rights give us no claim to income higher than what we need to live on, to a luxury apartment or to a luxury car.

Does an employer violate my human rights when he gives me work which I do not like? No, because I entered into a contract with my employer, and freely committed myself to fulfil the tasks set out in the contract which I accepted. If the employer abides by the contract, he can enforce it against me. But if he breaches it, I can sue and resign.

Admittedly, depending on the health of the economy and the employment market, the opportunity to resign may be illusory. Indeed, it is possible that I am so reliant on my employer that he can do whatever he wants with me. If the employer or the owner of my flat abuses his power, if he exploits my weak position and degrades my self-esteem, then he may, in an extreme case, also violate elementary human rights.

4

The Monopoly on Force

Only the state has the right to use force to achieve its goals. When skinheads beat up foreigners, the culprits have to be punished. The police, for their part, must protect foreigners. To do this, they must be able to use force against such brutal rabble-rousers where necessary. Only the police have the right to use such sanctions. As their use of force and compulsion is both allowed by the system and is necessary, people who are subjected to this force must be given special protection. Those who are abused or tortured in prison cannot simply "resign" or leave their "workplace". They therefore need much more effective protection than the employee from his employer. Employers or landlords must hold their own against their competitors. When they misuse their position they must justify their actions to unions, the media and the public. In a lonely prison cell, by contrast, sadistic prison guards or police can work off their aggression on someone who is helpless.

The state and its officials consequently occupy a special position in our legal system. They administer the so-called monopoly on force, that is, the sole right to use force in order to enforce the laws of the state. This special position must be subjected to special scrutiny. The state can prohibit conduct and impose sanctions on people against their will. In a free society no-one else may do this. It is because we are dependent on the

state that we must be given special protection against the
misuse of force by the state.

The authorities responsible for criminal prosecutions
must have the right to complete their work. But people are
handed over to them for better or worse and these people are
particularly vulnerable, for those who can rule over others
unchecked tend to misuse their power. We know from
experience that almost every person, deep inside them, has the
need to let others feel their power, when they are not super-
vised or scrutinised. We know all too well the official who
keeps us waiting at the counter because we are dependent on
his form or signature; the university professor who has no time
for certain students; the teacher who ignores unpopular
students, never asking them a question in class; or the head of
the authority who processes the applications of some particularly slowly or fobs them off by telephone because they dare to
interrupt what she was doing to ask her something.

When people are particularly dependent on the
bureaucracy – for example because they could be deported to
another country by the immigration authorities, where they
will possibly be tortured, or because the police can gain
entrance to their apartment by force, or because they must
silently watch how the procedure for the issue of a driver's
licence is drawn out arbitrarily – a constitutional democracy
must set up systems to keep authorities from misusing their
power. In such cases people have to defend themselves. For
instance, they must be able to protect themselves by appealing
to an independent court.

It is also possible for the government to misuse its
political power through its control of the executive to get rid of
unwelcome opposition. A government can instruct the police,
in relation to annoying political adversaries, to be particularly
alert, critical and strict, even to treat them poorly. When the

government, in addition to this, can rely on a private army of thugs, the police may even turn a blind eye to criminal actions taken against annoying adversaries.

If a climate of hate and violence has developed the government can bring the mass media, the press, even private businesses, industry and unions under its control, in order to consolidate its power and eliminate the opposition. Then it will find enough servile supporters in parliament to approve laws with which particular minorities can be oppressed. If this happens, courts will only be able to protect the rights of such people, that is, those of the minority, in a limited way.

A police commander of a canton in Switzerland acted against the instructions of the Swiss Federal Parliament in order to protect the human rights of Jews persecuted in Germany. These refugees from Germany were facing certain death in the concentration camps. The police commander saved their lives by falsifying their entry papers, and was convicted of breaching official regulations. Neither judges nor any other institution, until recently, was prepared to reopen the matter and acquit the police commander, to restore his honour as a tribute to him and to his family. The statutes of Switzerland obviously still count for more than the elementary humanity enshrined in inviolable human rights, which every state and every lawmaker should observe.

Human rights are thus rights which give people the instruments, the means, the potential and the ability to protect their established rights in the courts. The more powerful these courts are, the more independently they work and the more accessible they make themselves, the better human rights are protected in that country.

5

The History of Human Rights

150 years ago the German Parliament, the *Reichtstag*, drafted a catalogue of human rights. To complete this task, the Parliament wanted to give the *Kaiser* or emperor democratic legitimacy by giving him the Crown itself. The *Kaiser* refused: a *Kaiser*, the *Kaiser by divine grace, cannot* be offered a Crown by a Parliament elected by the people!

The kings of the Middle Ages saw themselves as rulers by divine grace, as rulers who governed the people in the service of God. Every act of state was taken in the name of God. In a system like this, where someone makes rules by divine grace, there is no room for human rights. The king is sovereign and is not subject to the judiciary.

The idea that people have inviolable rights is found in many philosophies and cultures. The entrenchment of human rights in a written document first occurred in the famous English Magna Carta of 1215. Despite the declaration of their belief in human rights, the princes, with their "right to rule", never allowed themselves to be restrained. They always expressed the view that human rights would be best protected when overseen by the princes themselves.

Yet the basic idea underlying the modern understanding of human rights is that it is the government that needs to be reminded of its duty to observe human rights. Human rights mark the boundary of the power of the state. They put a limit on the power of the legislature and require the government to respect human dignity even when this is unpleasant for the government. This obligation – and this is essential to human rights – should be enforceable by independent courts. Judges should be able to put even the head of state in her place, if she flouts human rights.

Clearly when we understand human rights as real rights, they must be left to the protection of judges. For a right is only a right if a court can establish its content, scope and boundary, as well as making the necessary decisions to safeguard it.

In the British Empire of the 17th century the first liberal king came to the throne by way of a bloodless revolution. Together with his parliament, he publicly affirmed a catalogue of human rights; the Bill of Rights of 1689. This became the basis for all later human rights declarations, commencing with the American Declaration of Independence of 1776, the Declaration of the Rights of Man of the French Revolution, the Bill of Rights of the American Constitution, up to the modern human rights declarations of the United Nations and Council of Europe.

With the written entrenchment of human rights came fundamental changes to the position of head of state. Whoever wants to rule in the name of the people must recognise that citizens have elementary, inviolable rights that even the government may not violate. From where do people get their right of revolution and their right to appoint a government? The fact that the people have elementary rights means that they have the right to appoint a new government. If the people did not have rights, they could never justify their *right* to judge the state and government.

The democratisation of state power heralded the triumphal march of human rights, at least on paper. Since the beginning of this age there has been no revolution in which the authority and the abuse of power of exploiters was not challenged in the name of human rights. Human rights undoubtedly also have their origins in the various democratic revolutions which, since the 17th century, have toppled one absolutist government after another.

The idea of human rights, for which so many people have sacrificed their lives, cannot be erased. Even if human rights are frequently abused, the idea of human rights ensures that national and international institutions continually try to translate rights which are guaranteed on paper into reality. Thus human rights ultimately have had a major influence on the fate of today's democratic states.

Human rights reflect the Enlightenment view of Man. The Enlightenment is the basis of modern democracies. "Enlightened" human beings individually can use their Reason to take their fate into their own hands. Each human being is her own "sovereign", and may not be forced by any state authority to adopt a different form of Reason than that which she perceives as correct. This view of human nature became the basis for later revolutions and democracy movements of the 18th and 19th centuries.

Of course a thinking person can still make mistakes. However, the mistake may not be corrected with state sanctioned force. Rather, we must assume that in a conflict between differing views and opinions the correct and more valuable opinion will prevail. In economic competition, as well as the unimpeded rivalry of opinion, the best always prevails because there is ultimately an "invisible hand" which ensures that in open competition the best comes to the forefront.

Towards the end of the 19th century, Marxism, and with it the communist party, shaped a totally different view of human nature which fundamentally changed the position of human rights. According to this view the human is an uprooted, alienated being, who is exploited through property and production. The exploited and alienated human being cannot recognise what is good for him. Left to himself, he will misuse his freedom for his own egotistical interests rather than use it for the good of all.

Therefore a human being must first be changed so that she can actually reason correctly. That there can be no human rights in this transitional period is clear. The task of the state, rather, is to change people in such a way that they can use their freedom "rationally". The human being should be "forced into freedom", until she can take her fate into her own hands. With such justifications human beings are dehumanised in the name of human rights in order to prepare for some future social paradise.

Different theories have divided humans into classes and made "superior human beings" out of some, such as the "Aryans" in national-socialist Germany. These theories have lead to the worst distortions of humanity. Thus Nazi Germany set itself the goal of eradicating the entire Jewish people, because they were considered inferior, indeed dangerous for humanity. The Slavic people were ranked somewhat higher. They were admittedly also seen as second-rate; for this they would be spared extermination only to be exploited as servants.

There can only be human rights when you recognise that all people are ultimately equal.

The resettlements and ethnic cleansing at the start and end of our century are the worst deformities of an absolutist territorial nationalism which only recognises human beings as a part of a nation. Such nationalism nips the civil right to freedom in the bud for the sake of a collective which has to do the thinking for all, lays down conclusive moral values for everybody and emasculates the individual common sense of human beings.

Individualist and collectivist ideologies are irreconcilably opposed to each other. Individualist ideologies see in each individual and his Reason the last sovereign authority which can distinguish correct from incorrect, true from false and good from bad. Confronted with this Reason, state power finds its limits. Collectivist ideologies, in contrast, convince themselves that only the state knows what is true, right and good, so that it can justify forcing human beings to see the "truth".

6

Why Do We Need Human Rights?

Example 1

A few years ago the Swiss Federal Court decided that the men in a particular canton could no longer deny women the right to vote and the right to run for political office. The right of men and women to equal treatment is such an elementary human right that it must be promoted by the courts even against the will of a professed majority.

Example 2

For decades American children of black parents were discriminated against in their schools and educational opportunities. They were taught in schools specially set up for black people. Then in the early 1950s the American Supreme Court decided that the policy of separate schooling actually led to discrimination against the black minority in the education system and therefore white and black children were to be taught together.

Example 3

A few years ago, in Switzerland, Mrs Belilos was fined because the police alleged that she had participated in an illegal demonstration. Although the former husband of the divorced woman could swear to the fact that at the time of the incident she was with him in a restaurant, where he was paying her maintenance for their children, the police insisted that they had seen her at the demonstration. There was no independent court in Switzerland that could have cleared up who was right. The police commission was confident that the police were to be believed, rather than an accused demonstrator. So the police stood by the fine. As the accusations had not been heard by a court, the fine was overturned by the European Court of Human Rights. Everyone has to have a fair chance to put their position before an independent court which can examine the issues without being influenced by the police.

Example 4

A young family fled from the war zone of Yugoslavia to Switzerland. The father was an officer in the Yugoslavian army. He was of Serbian descent, and his wife was of Croatian descent. Hence he did not want to fight in an army which would make him shoot his wife's brothers. Then the Croatian authorities decided they wanted to enlist the conscientious objector to Serbian military service in the Croatian army. In the Croatian army he would have had to fight against his own family.

Without the decision of a court, the women in the Swiss canton today would still not have the right to vote or run for office; without the decision of a court, black people in the United States would still have to send their children to "schools of apartheid"; without a court of human rights, Mrs Belilos would have to pay a fine for a crime she never committed.

Because the right to asylum is not a recognised human right, the family from the former Yugoslavia cannot expect that they will be able to prevail against the bureaucracy in their search for asylum.

Although people can protect themselves from arbitrary rule, we need human rights to protect minorities from discrimination by the majority. Courts must ensure that minorities can be protected from majorities. Women who do not have the right to vote and who are denied this right by a voting majority of men can only gain their rights by the decision of a court. Black people who are discriminated against by the majority of whites can only protect themselves with the help of legal action. The democratic lawmaker can hardly be convinced by human rights arguments; he will only want whatever reflects the political interests of the majority. The court, by contrast, cannot decide according to the division of political power.

Decisions of courts are only convincing when they employ rational arguments. If there are clear arguments why black children are impermissibly discriminated against by separate schools, the court must find in favour of the discriminated minority. *The human right protects the minority because it is entrusted to the courts.*

Mrs Belilos, convicted of a crime she never committed, would have had no chance to overturn the judgment, if it was not for an international European court of human rights which can protect her rights against Switzerland. The limitation of state power through international law is only possible because human rights belong to the recognised values of a democratic constitutional order. The protection afforded by international law is today still very rudimentary. However, in certain cases it has already proved its worth. If there were no human rights, nobody could go to the European court in order to enlist its assistance against the state.

There is no human right to asylum recognised in international law. The family from the former Yugoslavia consequently has no chance to obtain asylum through the application of a generally recognised principle of international law. There is also no human right that frees me from the duty to fight against relatives, and nothing which frees me from military service for my state.

7

Should People Govern the Law or Should the Law Govern People?

The remark of the absolutist French King Louis XIV "I am the state" has sounded through history. Are the states, democracies, rulers and the majority of the people above the law, or are they too bound by law? Can the French President simply declare that, due to vital national defence interests, France must conduct nuclear tests on Mururoa-Atoll, even when the population of the Pacific sees this as an indefensible infringement of their rights?

Recently the councils of the Swiss Confederacy conducted a citizens' initiated referendum, aimed at giving the authorities the power to deport without trial asylum-seekers who had illegally entered the country. The authorities would have been given the power to deport asylum-seekers to countries in which they faced gruesome forms of torture. International law prohibits states from deporting people in these circumstances. Every human being should have the right to protection from torture, and no state may expel human beings to states where they will be tortured. Can the Swiss Federal Constitution, by way of citizens' initiated referenda, not only entitle but require authorities to breach human rights? Are the people above the law?

One of the most important achievements of the Enlightenment was the conviction that states and governments are bound by the inalienable rights of the people. States can indeed create new laws, but they are not above the law. States are institutions created by law and a legal order. They only exist as a result of law. Hence they cannot change the law according to whim, or flout elementary human rights on account of professed "reasons of state".

Governments are bound by law. They can neither place themselves above it nor arbitrarily change it. There are inalienable human rights which states, whether large or small, poor or rich, strong or weak, democratic or dictatorial, may neither repeal nor violate. This even applies to the constituent authority which bestows the constitution on the state. Even where, by way of a revolution or national strike, the constitution is purportedly totally repealed and replaced with a new one, this does not entitle the constituent bodies of the state arbitrarily to circumvent human rights.

With the introduction of constitutional democracy, princes and kings were not just replaced by the rule of the people. No; with the founding of constitutional democracy the people were to be ruled by law.

If you look at the world today, you have to concede that few nations abide by this principle. Nevertheless, the commitment to and realisation of the idea of constitutional democracy, particularly when understood as the "rule of law" as it applies in the Anglo-Saxon legal tradition, have been essential for humanity's chance for peaceful survival.

If nations, in the name of democracy, revolt against the law, they will recklessly defend themselves against those who dispute their rights. This leads unintentionally to conflicts on both a small and large scale. Only the idea that even nations and states exist in and through law gives human rights any chance in particular states and against particular nations.

But who guarantees the proper application of rights? Political authorities? Neither the government nor the parliament can reliably guarantee the observance of the law. For the law erects barriers against state interests. There is no doubt that the barriers created by law can best be enforced by independent judges. The courts must guarantee the public that they will be "blind" to the majority as well as the minority; that is, that they will not be influenced by either side and will only be guided by laws that bind, even though they were passed by, the state.

8

The Separation of Powers and Human Rights

In a totalitarian country two students, Stefan and Anna, denounce their President. The school-principal expels them from school without warning. That school-principal is chosen by the President and can be sacked without reason. For the sake of his family, he had to be as submissive as possible towards the President.

The decision is challenged by the parents of the students in the Administrative Court. They say that the other students falsely accused their children. The parents are known to be notorious critics of the regime. And so the President, who has heard of the case, summons the judges, to make it clear what sort of decision is expected of them. As the judges in turn can be sacked by the President at any time, they will think twice before they impartially uphold the law, instead of trying to meet the expectations of the President.

If the constitution of this country had a strict separation of powers, the President would not be able to use power like this to interfere in the administration of justice or to force judges to make a particular decision. For example, thanks to the Constitution, judges of the American Supreme Court cannot be removed from office. They are elected for life. Indeed, the

United States' Constitution even says that salaries of the judges cannot be reduced during their period in office.

Separation of powers means that the different organs of the state, such as president and government, parliament and lawmaker as well as the judiciary, must be fundamentally independent from each other. Every institution should be able to make decisions independently of the others. If this was not the case, then the strongest and most powerful organ of the state – and this is usually the government – would be able to bring all the other institutions under its control. It could ensure that, for instance, judges apply constitutional and human rights only in the interests of the head of state, thereby for all practical purposes eroding them.

Even where they are explicitly guaranteed by the constitution, human rights can be annulled in practice when there is no separation of powers. And if a President can also issue decrees which possess the force of law, few are safe from absolutist power. For instance, such a President could, at any time, issue a ruling making all criticism of the President punishable by law.

If, furthermore, a President also has the courts under control, he can misuse power to meet personal interests. A President could use the secret police, subject neither to statutory limitations nor to judicial scrutiny, to spy on everybody and to eliminate political opponents.

The idea that the basic principle of the separation of powers is not just a question of good governance (as is, for example, the specialisation of labour) but also protects the freedom of citizens, was developed by the two great state-theorists of the Enlightenment, Locke and Montesquieu, as early as the 17th and 18th centuries. Montesquieu recognised in his classic, *The Spirit of the Laws*, that there can only be freedom and human rights in a state when state power is divided and the different organs of the state operate as mutual checks and balances.

The Limits of the Separation of Powers

The separation of powers itself has not been realised to the same extent in every state. Some years ago, there were serious allegations of police misconduct in Queensland, Australia. Amongst other things, some people complained that the police were treating demonstrators unfairly. Eventually, the State Government and Parliament set up a commission to investigate the police. In order effectively to protect citizens from police misconduct in the future, the legislature had to be able to authorise the inquiry to examine files held by the executive, and to question both the police and other members of the executive.

The executive could not invoke the separation of powers. This case was not a matter of maintaining the independence of the police from the legislature. Rather, it was concerned with the scrutiny and, if need be, the limits on the power of the executive imposed by the legislature.

Something similar happened on the federal level in the United States in the famous "Iran-Contra Affair". The National Security Council, protected by the separation of powers, secretly diverted the proceeds of the sale of arms to Iran to a group of rebels in Nicaragua, known as the Contras. This was contrary to United States law. The full extent of these activities only came to light thanks to inquiries by congressional select committees. But Congress managed to do this only because it could compel information to be given to it. Such compulsion is only possible if one institution can, in effect, infringe the rights of the other. This in turn is only possible when the separation of powers is not seen simply as a clear division of institutions, but is understood as a principle of mutual checks and balances.

9

On the Universality of Human Rights

In Turkey recently a representative of the people was expelled from parliament because she allegedly either directly or indirectly supported a separatist terrorist organisation, the PKK ("for an autonomous Kurdistan"). In a short trial that was highly criticised in the media she was given a long prison sentence.

For the protection of their own parliamentarians the Inter-parliamentary Union commissioned a delegation to investigate if and to what extent human rights had been violated in this trial. In Turkey it was made clear to the delegation that their concern for human rights ultimately threatened and challenged the Turkish state. The Turkish state was said to be defined in the Constitution as a unitary state. It was said that this constitutional provision would always be in force and could not be changed; it was imperative to the survival of the state. It was asserted that whoever challenges the unity of the Turkish state damages vital interests of that society.

Many representatives of Turkey accuse the West of hypocrisy in denouncing human rights violations. They argue that the West's own violations of human rights, such as the treatment of terrorists in police jails or the discrimination against Native Americans in the United States, go relatively unnoticed, while the desperate battle of the Turkish state against Kurdish separatism on the one hand and Islamic fundamentalism on the other is denounced in the Western media.

Turkey accuses the West of using the issue of human rights to discredit non-Western states: the issue of human rights as an instrument of neo-colonialism. But the universality of human rights themselves is also under challenge. Turkey invokes its particular cultural tradition, which is said to force upon it a particular understanding and relationship with human rights.

Only those who acknowledge the sovereignty of each person will also ascribe to him individual human rights with which to challenge, if necessary, the interests of the collective. But those who claim that the interests of the collective, here the interests of the Turkish state, are more important than individual human rights will find it difficult to avoid the conclusion that the right to freedom of expression should be restricted, for the sake of the preservation of Turkish unity.

Undoubtedly, it is not possible to say at present that rights to intellectual liberty, such as freedom of the press, freedom of expression and perhaps also freedom of worship and conscience, are universally accepted as human rights in an individualist sense. This will only become possible when the Western world, together with other cultural traditions, acknowledges the existence of collective values. However, we must not allow collective rights to be misused to cripple individual human rights. A person's dignity is not just an individual matter: it also depends on the kind of society to which he belongs and his place in that society. This, however, does not entitle the collective to disregard the value of the individual completely, nor to justify undermining him in the interest of the whole.

There is no room for compromise over elementary human rights, such as physical integrity, human dignity and the prohibition of gruesome punishment. Every violent intrusion through torture or mutilation must be denounced as a violation of physical integrity. Furthermore, appealing to a particular culture or tradition as justification for accused criminals to be convicted and sentenced on the basis of flimsy evidence is as unconvincing as the claims of Islamic law for the practice of particularly drastic forms of corporal punishment.

Are human rights a luxury which poor states cannot afford? It may be true that in the interests of the development of a country the collective should be accorded more rights than the lone individual. However, elementary human rights, such as protection of human dignity and the preservation of physical integrity, may not be disregarded, even in such a context: poverty excuses neither state-terrorism nor torture.

10

How Can Human Rights be Realised and Protected?

If someone could give a valid answer to this question, they would quickly be showered with peace prizes. The fight for the better protection of human rights is as old as the violation of elementary human rights itself. *If you want to protect human rights you must limit the power that people have over others and ensure that this power is subject to continual scrutiny.* However, this very requirement shows how difficult it is to achieve this goal. Man, said the philosopher Thomas Hobbes more than 300 years ago, is addicted to either power, honour or money. He behaves so as to maintain or increase his power; he seeks honour and glory in politics, sport, science, the church or art, or he slaves away, trying to acquire economic power and prestige. These characteristics are just as congenital to Mankind as the need for security, for affection and for friendly social co-existence.

If you want to minimise the violation of human rights, you cannot ignore reality: only if you are open to all facets of human potential can you design institutions and processes that can prevent human rights violations and ensure the scrutiny of those who exercise power over others. The police officer who interrogates a prisoner must be restrained. So must the leader of a state who has to decide if rebellious minorities should be treated with the stick and the carrot, or just the stick.

In both cases, there are those who object to restraint and to the improved protection of human rights on the grounds that restraint is completely against the interests of citizens who want to be protected against terrorists and murderers. Every concession to terrorists is interpreted as weakness on the part of the government. Revolutions and civil wars are said to be the consequences of a "soft" government which sees the protection of human rights as their last chance to preserve power in a state which has not been legitimate in the eyes of the people for a long time.

Distrust of human rights protection and the effective restraint of state power is always stirred up by the powerful. Authoritarian governments are not afraid of terrorists, but they are afraid of the opposition that can only be silenced, so they believe, by state-terror. Particularly in times of tension, it is essential to remember that ultimately a government can only be confident that it will not be toppled by force if it is able to give collegial acknowledgment of the other side, real attention to their arguments, serious negotiation in the interests of all affected and a readiness and ability to compromise. In the long term no government can base its peace on bayonets.

Parliaments and governments which want to prevent the development of a civil war atmosphere have to assure their people that they can criticise their state and their government and articulate their needs and frustrations, and that the proper authorities, and not just the opposition, will listen to them, take their problems into account and respond to them.

Along with the mutual checks on power, states and public authorities also have to be able to learn. But states are only able to learn if they have institutions in which not only the established majorities of the land assert themselves, but political, religious, linguistic, social and cultural minorities can do so as well and are listened to. This requires sensible voting systems, strengthening of the media and the prevention of media monopolies, regular election of new parliamentarians, the scrutiny of political parties in states with a parliamentary democracy and, ultimately, constitutional procedures which enable a government to be changed through democratic constitutional processes, on the basis of rational and reasonable dialogue.

Finally, *federalism and decentralisation* should, just like the separation of powers, contribute to minimising the dangers of abuse of power by people who have political power. If those who exploit power sit in inaccessible centralised bureaucracies, the ordinary citizen has absolutely no chance to raise concerns with the government. But if people deal with a public authority or small municipality in which they might know someone, they will find out where and how to express their concerns faster, simply and without tedious bureaucracy.

The idea of human rights, however, must also become part of the political and social culture. In an atmosphere of mutual tolerance, in a society which upholds the value of human dignity and freedom, and in a political system that is used to living with either changing majorities or stability, human rights have a better chance than in a society ruled by hate and intolerance, where every party is either an outright winner or loser.

For this reason human rights have to be included in the education and school system. "Do unto others as you would have others do unto you." This is the fundamental ethical principle of all human rights. If school children can be won over to this elementary principle, then they will be much more prepared, especially as adults with insight and understanding, to lend their support to the realisation and improvement of human rights in society and politics.

Any member of parliament, of a public authority or even of a government, who as a child in school was not acquainted with the idea of human rights, will greet demands for improved protection of human rights with greater suspicion than someone who has grown up with the culture of human rights. Public authorities often see a hidden criticism of past activities in demands for stronger protection of human rights. If, however, discussions about human rights are part of normal social life, then public authorities will be more open-minded and ready to respond to growing demands for human rights. The chances that human rights will be realised and can be asserted grow when human rights belong to the every-day.

Finally, existing international law protects human rights in a limited way in states which have acceded to the relevant conventions. In so far as these conventions establish independent judicial bodies, such as the European Court of Human Rights in Strasbourg, they contribute markedly to the improvement of human rights situations in states that already have a developed judicial system and mechanisms for monitoring human rights violations.

However, in so far as these instruments contribute to the politicisation of international human rights and are seen by some as a means for undermining the authority of a weak government, and by others as a means for asserting their own economic interests, they contribute little to the improvement of the human rights situation and are detrimental to further development.

International law is only useful in so far as it helps to convince the public authorities of a state that they themselves have to contribute to the better protection of human rights in that country. In this capacity international conventions for the protection of human rights are certainly sensible. However, which public authority is prepared to relinquish power and impose limits on itself in the interests of human rights? Public authorities need lengthy and sympathetic arguments before being convinced to take such measures. The international commitment to human rights needs patience, perseverance and readiness to accept repeated setbacks.

11

Majority Rule in a Democracy and Human Rights

Democracy and freedom are Siamese twins. The one cannot exist without the other. The people – that is, all the citizens – could rise against those who ruled "by divine grace", the kings, princes and emperors, only because they believed in the ability of human beings, when in a majority, to decide what serves the good of the people better than the rulers. Popular sovereignty has its roots in the "sovereignty" of the individual citizen, who as a being endowed with Reason can independently decide about the justice of the laws. This belief in humans as beings endowed with Reason who can make decisions for themselves is a indispensable precondition of modern democratic society.

Furthermore, only in a democratically organised state do citizens have the institutions, courts and the necessary authority with which they can effectively scrutinise government abuses of power. An example: in the United States more than 20 years ago, some Republicans broke into the "sanctum" of the Democratic Party, the Watergate Hotel, to get secret information about the electoral strategy of their opponents and to further the ends of their presidential candidate at the time, Richard Nixon. It was only thanks to the press and the democratic system of the United States that it was possible for this scandal to be brought to the attention of the general public. When the inquiry into the affair took place, the investigating authorities had to obtain audio tapes from President Nixon on which the telephone conversations of the incumbent Head of State were recorded.

A lower district court finally decided, in a decision that would be unthinkable on the European continent, to compel the President to hand over the incriminating audio-tapes. The President could not invoke the importance of his office before the "lower" district judge. He had to hand over the tapes, otherwise he could have been punished by the court.

This subordination of the head of state to the superiority of the lower district court judge bears witness to an amazingly deep respect for justice and demonstrates the democratic self-understanding of a state that can distinguish between the office and the person. If a person misuses his official capacity he must be treated in the same way as all other citizens, irrespective of this capacity.

However, human rights are not protected in every democracy. The masses can be led through propaganda and hate-campaigns to oppress minorities. That is how a democracy can destroy itself. Democracy destroys the rule of law when it gives an ethnic or racial majority the ability to use the state solely in its own service, as happened in Nazi Germany.

The governments of communist states, through highly controversial electoral rules and the oppression of political opposition, were also repeatedly rewarded for their past achievements with 90 – 99% of votes. In the nation-states of Eastern Europe which were formed after the collapse of the Communist Party, majorities have often adopted new constitutions to the detriment of minorities. The minorities deny the state their loyalty because they are convinced that these constitutions only serve the interests of the national majority, and that the constitutions, though democratically endorsed, are designed to give the majority rights and instruments for discriminating against the minority. That is why the minorities demand new procedures and rights so that they can found their own state. This almost insoluble dilemma was first created by the belief in a democracy which appears always to support the majority.

But if democracy only ever supports the same majority, and if the majority in turn abuses its rights in order to discriminate against minorities, freedom is undermined by democracy. In this case the media are put to the service of the majority too, stirring its animosity towards minorities, who may be asylum-seekers, black people, or members of other nations.

A new version of "us and them", that justifies terror and every violation of human rights, always turns the majority and the minority into warring communities. So democratic majority-rule, particularly in multicultural states with clearly distinguishable majorities and minorities, leads to state sanctioned and social discrimination. Democracy is then only really a democracy for the ethnic majority. The state uses democratic constitutional dress as a disguise that serves as "sheep's clothing" to conceal degrading discrimination against minorities.

However, democracy should not be understood as simply meaning majority-rule. For the majority cannot always be in the right. *Human rights, for example, can never be sacrificed for the interests of the majority.* Democracy only serves freedom if it gives the subordinated minority a real chance and hope to one day achieve a majority. This, however, can only happen if open dialogue is possible in the relevant state.

The majority is not infallible just because it won the election or voted. Naturally it is easier to arrive at the truth when many join in the search for truth or agree on a decision.

However, these truths are always merely relative. There are no pearls of wisdom that are irrefutable and infallible just because the democratic sovereign found them. They too have to prove their worth on the touchstone of Reason, of constitutional democracy and of human rights. Finally, they are valid only until they can no longer be changed by a new majority. If it is no longer possible for minorities to hope to have open dialogue with the majority and to convince them of other truths, democracy and majority-rule lose their justification.

Democracy as the path to freedom today is primarily endangered because the opinion of voters can be manipulated by the mass-media (especially where there is media monopoly) in a manner that was never thought possible in the past. Voters must be able to get a true picture of the goals and intentions of the relevant political parties. As long as there are no alternatives offered, as long as political goals and intentions cannot publicly be criticised, scrutinised and compared, democracy is a sham. If people are indoctrinated through the media with views to which no-one would freely admit, if cheap emotional propaganda and the spread of half-truths hinder voters from being able to form their own opinions, then the mass media has eroded freedom and democracy.

Ultimately democracy can be the twin sister of freedom only if it gives as many people as possible the opportunity to win over a majority in the community to their cause. Democracy thus has to be understood as a procedure that secures the right to self-determination for the largest possible number in the state community. It has to be understood primarily as a process for making decisions which under given conditions, and in the relevant social setting, best allow for self-determination.

The search for consensus with a large minority reflects the spirit of democracy understood from the perspective of the right to self-determination. If you understand democracy in this sense, as a system of state-organisation that ensures the largest possible degree of self-determination, then democracy has a very close relationship with individual human rights. Looked at in this way, democracy is the expression of individual human rights, because where humans, as social beings, can no longer make decisions just for themselves individually, democracy gives the largest possible number the chance to take part in decisions that affect the community.

How does the democratic state ensure self-determination for the largest possible number other than through majority-rule? If democratic decisions are decentralised, if, for example, every local council democratically could make decisions, then many in the state could make decisions for themselves. That is why in order to make extensive self-determination possible, federalist states have supplemented the democratic system through a federal system. The principle of maximising self-determination is realised through the democratic autonomy of local public bodies.

12

Courts are the Best Protection

A few years ago the Western media cheered the Russian President Gorbachev. He was regarded as a model of a good, far-seeing and just statesman. His opposite number at the time, Yeltsin, was ostracised and marginalised. Yeltsin had only just cleared the hurdle of a democratic election when Western opinion changed its view of him. Then he became celebrated as the statesman who was in a position to introduce Western values into a decaying Russian society. Hardly anyone took exception to Yeltsin using blood and canon to realise his goals by removing the parliamentary supporters of a putsch. The main point was that an elected president with the good intention of establishing a democratic constitution should not be allowed to be hindered in this aim by former fellow travellers and communists.

Furthermore, hardly anyone was bothered by the fact that Yeltsin let only a very small band of supporters draw up his constitution, that he then presented it to the people without parliamentary approval and that the constitution, probably, was never approved by the required threshold of 50% of voters.

In the West people marvelled at the new "democratic" constitution of the Russian Federation. They deliberately overlooked the fact that the new Russian President, in practice, held the power of the American President (the right to veto laws), together with those of the French President (the right to issue decrees and the right to appoint a government) as well as those of the Czars from the time of the post-1905 Duma (the right to legislate).

Yeltsin was celebrated as a statesman. As the first major conflicts between nationalities, such as those in Chechnya, cast a shadow over the young democracy, people suddenly began to doubt, not the constitution, but President Yeltsin as a person. Yeltsin was no longer the magnificent statesman people had taken him to be a few months earlier. It was only when forced to reckon with the fact that an extreme right-wing fascist and nationalist could become president in the next election that doubt crept in about the value of the system itself.

This phenomenon of confusing persons and institutions is not new. It still reflects our current thinking to a large extent. We dream even today of the good fairy-tale king who benevolently rules over the people. Where there are fairy-tale kings there need be no human rights. For they do everything to defend the weak against the strong. Do not such archetypes still dominate the world of our imagination?

Are human rights best protected by good, wise, or even priestly statesmen and stateswomen? Or is it institutions that ultimately can ensure the effective protection of human rights?

Because human beings recognise that they are by nature quarrelsome and violent, they freely and in their own interests submit themselves to an order that regulates how people can acquire power, honour and money. This order, says the English philosopher Hobbes, is run by a state with a ruler who is equipped with unlimited power.

Hobbes, mind you, never asked himself this question: to what extent are the people that run this superstate (ie the rulers), also addicted to corruption, glory, domination and money and, for this reason, prepared to undermine the values of the society, to serve their own interests? History since Hobbes has given us some terrifying examples of such reckless, power-obsessed rulers in the form of Hitler, Stalin, Idi Amin or even Pol Pot.

The English historian Lord Acton (1834-1902) once made a remark born of great wisdom and experience: "Power tends to corrupt and absolute power corrupts absolutely". Such insight into the reality of human nature is undoubtedly the basis for an understanding of human rights that entrusts these rights not to people, but to institutions. Whoever has a little power over others will, experience shows, misuse this power at some time, if it is not checked. He will oppress those with less power. Further, such people will try to expand their power over others and will do everything to remove possible competitors so as to achieve a monopoly on power.

This characteristic of human nature is just as innate as the desire for freedom, independence, opportunity for development and the satisfaction of needs. Anyone who wants to tailor-make a state constitution for human rights must create organisations of state that are made for so-called "good" governments. For experience shows that even the best governors, once they taste power for the first time, tend to abuse it. Indeed, human rights are best protected in a state when the institutions are designed so that people who wield power keep each other in check, in order to keep this inevitable weakness of human beings to a minimum. Checks and balances ensure that public authorities listen, inform themselves and adapt as well as learn. For the human being is by nature not only a being that is greedy for domination, glory and money. The human is also primarily a being that can learn. Institutions are good if they are tailored to accommodate ordinary, normal people as we know them from experience. We cannot have constitutions which envisage institutions that can only be run by and for "superior human beings".

The belief in the good Prime Minister or President or Premier who protects human rights with his own power is naive and overlooks the basic yearning of people for power. That is why, if human rights are important to us, we have to rely much more on sensible institutions. We need to consider which of these might limit the power of office-holders and at the same time force public authorities to inform themselves comprehensively and to learn from such information. We need to know which institutions, on the other hand, are too weak to efficiently counter the thirst for power of those who already have it.

Human rights are protected when they are entrusted to the institution of the court. This requirement does not reflect the naive belief that judges are better people than state presidents or prime ministers. Faith in judges is grounded in the institution and in the procedure of the court that fits the average person like no other. Experience shows that this institution, even when it is filled with mediocre people, is least in danger of being guided by interests of power because such interests are foreign to the institution and its procedures. The judge is only held in esteem if her judgments are justified rationally, that is, her decision can be understood by third parties. She has to decide, impartially, which of the arguments presented by the parties is convincing.

13

The Secret of the Fair Trial

Only visible justice is just

The Myer family is having a delicious strawberry tart for dessert. The two little ones, Christy and Sean, have to share the last piece. How should their mother divide the cake in order to treat the children as fairly as possible? She could divide up the slice of cake herself and try as hard as possible to cut pieces of the same size. The critical Christy would surely accuse her mother of giving Sean a larger piece than her and of treating them both unjustly.

The mother could also get Christy to divide the cake and give Sean the right to choose the first piece. Then she could be sure that Christy would take great care to cut equal pieces.

A good process often guarantees more justice than any standards set for the content of justice. The credibility of a process carried out in accordance with human rights standards depends on whether those affected take part in the process.

The process should give both parties before the court the same chance to convince independent judges of the merit of their view. Furthermore, it should ensure that the court is only allowed to find against someone when it is sure that it has found sufficient evidence to warrant this.

In order to apply a legal principle like *"those who kill should be punished with prison or restrained by procedures for the mentally-ill,"* two different procedural steps are necessary:

1   The court must know whether the accused killed the victim; that is, the court has to know the truth about the facts of the case;

2   It also has to be clear to the court which criminal norm is to be applied to this particular homicide; that is, it has to apply the law to the concrete facts of the case.

The first question is by far the most awkward. Which procedures can best guarantee that the court has found the truth? Are you, for instance, allowed to assume that the evidence of members of the police is, as such, more credible than that of private third parties? Are the authorities allowed to expel asylum-seekers to their country of origin without investigating the extent to which they are endangered in that country?

The legal system has to provide procedural rules that have the greatest chance, based on past experience and taking human fallibility into account, of getting as close as possible to the truth. "Truth", for example, that is only based on the testimony of one party is no truth. As age-old human experience shows, it is easiest to get to the true facts when you listen to all parties involved in the incident. Nobody is allowed to judge his own case, nobody is allowed to pass judgment before listening to all those affected.

However, those who are authorised to find the truth can feel that they "possess the truth". This sweeping authority often leads administrative authorities or judges to conclude their investigations prematurely based on preconceived opinions for reasons of convenience. The evidence of a third party that coincides with their assumptions receives more credibility than the evidence of witnesses that could undermine the whole structure of assumed facts. Such a process is far from credible. If elementary procedural rights are not built into the process, not only will the truth be neglected, but the fundamental human rights of those affected will be violated as well.

In the inquisitorial system which applies in some countries, both the court and the public prosecutor use their powers to search for the truth. This is because both the court and the Office of the Public Prosecutor are authorised and required to undertake their own investigations to search for the truth.

The judges of the Middle-Ages assumed that only the confession of the accused could be used as evidence of the truth. So public prosecutors and judges used torturers to help to wring confessions out of their victims. Are investigators allowed, in the course of their inquiries, to have full and absolute control over a person and her body? Is a suspect, including the inherent core of her being, totally at the mercy of judges and police? Are they allowed in the course of their inquiries to use torture to bring people to divulge their innermost secrets and sign confessions which they would never freely sign? Is not there an inherent core of self-esteem and personality which no-one is allowed to penetrate without the consent of those affected?

Is the court later allowed to use information that has been illegally obtained by the investigating authorities, obtained by illegal phone-tapping or bugging?

Are the investigating authorities allowed to do deals with those charged with crimes, so that they will testify as witnesses against others in exchange for a reduced sentence or even immunity? Is an informant whose testimony clinches the case allowed to stay anonymous in order to protect him from acts of reprisal?

In contrast to the criminal trials of continental Europe, in trials coming out of the Anglo-Saxon tradition the courts and in particular the jurors are, so to speak, blind. The courts are not allowed of their own initiative to undertake any investigative tasks to help them reach a verdict; they can only work with the information provided to them by the parties. Truth, in the eyes of the adversarial system, is that which the parties can best prove to the court. The trial is a competition in which the best party is supposed to win. This picture, particularly in criminal proceedings, at first glance is thoroughly objectionable from the continental European point of view. Can we and are we allowed to talk of competition between the parties when the issues at hand are murder and manslaughter?

On the other hand, human experience shows that such proceedings are much less vulnerable to use as state-run show trials, that it is next to impossible to use such proceedings to silence political opponents by way of mock-trials, and that such proceedings are the best protection against a miscarriage of justice.

Admittedly, the accused have to rely on competent, and expensive, lawyers. With good defence lawyers, an accused is much more likely to be acquitted than with bad lawyers. Truth thus becomes a market commodity. In such proceedings accused parties who are poor are faced with a miscarriage of justice. Statistics for the United States show, for example, that as a proportion of the respective populations, the number of black people convicted is on average far above that of whites.

Human rights in criminal proceedings should protect those detained during the investigation from unacceptable intrusions upon their integrity; they should ensure that nobody can be convicted on the basis of illegally obtained evidence and they should mean that the accused have a fair chance to present their point of view to the court.

But human rights are also relevant for the court. It has to have the highest credibility so that judgments, which can utterly change the life of an accused and can keep people in jail for years, are seen as justified. Impartiality, independence and careful investigation of the facts: these are the demands placed on courts to ensure a trial that will stand the test of human rights.

14

Are the Police All-Powerful?

Fourteen-year-old Maya was invited to a party by a girlfriend. She promised her parents to be home by eleven o'clock at the latest. But it was all so much fun that it was soon one o'clock in the morning and she could not get home by public transport. So she had to ride home on a bicycle, which she borrowed from her girlfriend.

In the middle of the city her back light went out and she was immediately stopped by the police. She naturally did not have her identity card with her. In many countries people are required to have their identity cards with them when they go out in public. When Maya was asked to prove that she had not stolen the bicycle, she panicked. Now the police were totally convinced that a young girl who rode around the city at such a late hour with a defective bicycle was suspicious. They arrested Maya and, in order to ascertain her identity, took her to the police station where she had to spend the night. She was not allowed to call her parents. The police were firmly convinced that Maya had ridden a stolen defective bicycle in the city after one o'clock in the morning, and that she was a well-known liar. Consequently, she had to spend the night at the police station without informing her relatives. Her anxious parents, who telephoned everywhere during the night, first learned of the fate of their daughter at nine o'clock the following morning.

Anyone who is on the streets, who cannot identify themselves and who looks suspicious can be taken to the police station in order to ascertain their identity. If this cannot be determined straight away, they will have to wait until the police have carried out the necessary inquiries.

In Anglo-Saxon countries this sort of police power is seen as an example of the lack of freedom in other states. In Anglo-Saxon countries the police can only intervene in order to protect other citizens from violence, and can never, even temporarily, take people into custody on the basis of mere conjecture and suspicion. Many Anglo-Saxons maintain that there is no real freedom on the European continent because the uncontrolled power of the police is so extensive.

The French Revolution not only made the state democratic, it also gave it a new task; the state became the instrument with which to make a modern, bourgeois, liberal civil society out of a feudal society. So that the government would not be hindered in this task by conservative judges, Napoleon removed the classic restraining role of judges through the creation of a particular type of law, that is, public law. That is how the bourgeois authoritarian state was created; a state which gives the government the necessary authority to reorganise society. The police are the extension of the government. They have to impose the policies of the lawmakers and executive on the people; if necessary, by force. They therefore need the relevant powers.

In contrast, the way the English see their police is totally different. Forty years ago my host-family at the time taught me what an English "bobby" is. If you do not know the time, if you do not know your way, even if you have toothache, you are supposed to ask the bobby for help. The way the

English see their police as their friend and helper was new to me who had been taught to respect and fear the police.

As the English police perform their duties without weapons they make a decisive contribution to this perception. Even if they were attacked they would have the vast majority of citizens on their side, as no-one can stand by when their own friend and helper is in trouble.

The government cannot give the police direct instructions to intervene. Such decisions have to be made by the "Chief Constable". If the Chief Constable does not accept the government's instructions, the instructions will not be binding on the police unless they are upheld by a court. The police are independent of the government because the government, as the majority-party, only ever represents a little over 50% of the population. The police, however, have to protect the entire population.

Consistent with this, the police also have no special sovereign power to fulfil their tasks. They can only arrest someone as a measure of last resort in order to protect others or themselves from violence. This is a different understanding of law, which does not see in public institutions an authority that imposes and realises particular ideologies and interests. According to this understanding the state is a mediator between conflicting social forces and interests. It has to prevent violence and act as the mediator between different parties to ensure that conflicts are dealt with through democratic dialogue and without violence.

In continental European states the population see the police in a totally different light. No-one wants to have anything to do with the police. The police serve as a bogeyman to threaten naughty children. They are a threat rather than an ever-ready helper. In fact, statutory regulations in Switzerland require the police to act in a way largely similar to that of the

English police. The English-style perception, however, has yet to gain acceptance. The sovereign powers of the police, judicial review of which is difficult, still go much further in continental Europe than they do in England.

Let's return to Maya and assume that, on the following day, Maya comes home, totally shocked by her imprisonment. It is only some time later that her mother forms the impression that Maya was raped during the night at the police station. Maya says nothing because she is too ashamed to say anything about it. Her mother, however, gradually becomes certain. How can she accuse the police? How can she prevent the police acting in the same way towards another girl?

Maya and her mother are to a large degree defenceless. For a start, the police have the trust of the judges and the authorities on their side. What is more, public law on the European continent today still does not allow courts to be used to enforce administrative measures, such as stronger scrutiny of the police or the prompt provision of information to parents.

In states with minorities who are discriminated against, the strong position of the police further weakens the oppressed. The police are there for the protection of citizens. But what happens when the police themselves treat minorities as second-class citizens? If the people receive only inadequate protection from the police they will become fair game for bands of racists which, because they have nothing to fear from the police, can act unhindered against minorities, using brutal violence, arson, death threats, continual harassment, accusations and slander with the secret support of the population. The police, who have to intervene for the protection of all, only give the impression that they are intervening, but soon let the perpetrators free once more.

We also accuse the police of inaction when they do not take effective steps to shut down a drug scene, or arrest rampaging demonstrators, or excise the ever growing cancer of organised crime. This is where the big dilemma of protection of human rights against the police becomes apparent. If the police are equipped with sweeping powers they are in danger of becoming a state within the state. If they are powerless the state and society are in danger of dissolving into anarchy. It is difficult to tread the path between the police-state and anarchy. That is why careful statutory regulations have to be supplemented by sound education and training of the police force, by members of those groups particularly affected joining the police force, and also by encouraging in the populace a new way of seeing the police.

It is often too easy to make the police responsible for all human rights violations without searching for the real causes. After all, human rights apply to the police as well!

15

Human Rights in the School and Education

Theo is a proud first-grader. He worships his teacher, who tells him things he has never heard from his parents before. That is why he suddenly starts to behave differently at home. He washes himself more often, he no longer shakes hands with anyone, he is frightened of contagious diseases of which he had previously never heard. He no longer speaks with his school mates, he swears at children who do not wash their hands after every meal, and he asks his parents to do the same as him. At night he has nightmares. He wakes bathed in sweat and dreams of evil people who continually persecute him. His parents find out that the teacher is an active member of an extreme religious sect, a controversial group due to its intolerant stance, and that she has set herself the goal of winning the children over to the ideals of the sect.

What can parents do in a case such as this? They naturally invoke their human rights, that is, their right to raise their child according to their own values. They invoke parental rights and the rights of the child. If children are allowed to be pressured to the extent that they feel they are in a world threatened by evil, their elementary opportunity to develop has been violated. The parents will therefore try to convince the education authorities that their parental rights entitle them to the human right to change little Theo's school.

The reply will come from the education authorities: the state can only fulfil its educational tasks and guarantee the right to a school-education if it is allowed certain freedoms in the organisation and running of schools. The parents have to accept that children will possibly come into contact with different values in schools than those imparted to them at home. In a pluralistic society parents have very different ideas about a sound education. That is why it is no longer possible for schools to impart a view of the world that fits all parents in the same way. Everyone has the human right to have their children educated in a private school. The human right to private education, however, is without substance and un-realistic, for next to no-one can afford to privately finance school education.

Perhaps the education authorities agree that the teacher exceeded her brief. They will therefore have to consider whether the teacher should be dismissed. In the case of dis-missal, mind you, the teacher will also invoke her human rights, that is, to freedom of association and personal freedom.

Who should now resolve the conflict: the court or the Education Department? If the Department decides then Theo's parents and the teacher, depending on the decision, will allege bias. If the parents lose it will be clear to them that the Depart-ment protects its teachers regardless of criticism. If the teacher loses she will accuse the Department of caving in to political pressure. In an election year it is understandable that politicians bow to the pressure of the street.

Only a judicial decision can claim credibility, precisely because judges are not interested in the outcome of the decision nor forced to reckon with the consequences of the decision if they decide in favour of the parent or the teacher.

Administrative authorities, on the other hand, often put up a fight against the sweeping powers of judges. Resolution by the court takes much too long, they object, it is much too bureaucratic and ultimately asks too much of the court. A court necessarily would make unworldly decisions when it has to reach a view on educational issues with which judges are not acquainted.

Despite these claims the best solution is to choose the lesser evil; that is, in this case, to let a court make the final decision. If both sets of human rights – those of the parents and those of the teacher – are to be taken seriously, an independent judicial authority must be able to make the decision. This is because only an independent court can credibly administer human rights and apply them to actual conflicts.

The question which, however, remains unanswered is by which principles the court should be guided, when, for example, different human rights, such as those of the teacher and those of the parents, come into conflict with each other. How does a court find its bearings when, on the one hand, the parents invoke their parental rights and, on the other, the Education Department invokes its authority to be solely responsible for the education of children?

In many international conventions, as well as constitutions, certain principles were developed to enable courts to resolve such conflicts. *For a start, constitutional and human rights may only be restricted by a political lawmaker.* Statutes dealing with schools which set out the basics of the school curriculum, regulations about the selection and dismissal of teachers and disciplinary rules about the duties of public servants are important authorities for this purpose. But even these statutory rules themselves can restrict human rights only to the extent required by the overwhelming public interest.

A legal ruling, for instance, that requires girls to come to school wearing the veil would be an indisputable breach of the human right to freedom of religion and conscience. But what about a law which says that people may not receive unemployment benefits if they cannot get a job because they refuse to work on Saturdays? This is an intrusion on the rights of those who believe that Saturday, not Sunday, is a holy day. When the legislature of South Carolina made a law like this, Mrs Shabert, who was a Seventh-Day Adventist, was refused unemployment benefits. Possible arguments to support the law were, for example, that it might discourage people without real religious beliefs from trying to take Saturday off and claiming unemployment benefits if they lose their jobs.

Now a court has to ask itself whether reasons like this are sufficient to force people who belong to minority religions to work on Saturday, given the right to freedom of religion and conscience. The court in this case asked whether there was a "compelling state interest" which would justify this intrusion into people's beliefs. If the intrusion is proportional, Seventh-Day Adventists will have to join the majority. If, as in this case, it is not, an exception will have to be created for them.

The decision about the conflict with the sect will have to be made in a similar way. If the child can change schools without major problems, then we will look for a pragmatic solution to the conflict. It is also possible that the teacher is prepared to restrict herself to pure teaching tasks and refrain from taking on educative roles that some parents find intrusive because they want to teach their children according to their own values.

All of this shows the importance which human rights can have for individuals. Even when no reference is made to them, human rights still can often be seen guiding our legislature, executive and judiciary.

16

Why Does a Murderer Have Human Rights?

Anyone who visits the High Court of Justice in Israel will be amazed by the many prisoners waiting in the hall to talk with a member of the High Court. They are all prisoners claiming the right of "habeas corpus". Just imagine a high court in some other countries where prisoners from the jails who want an audience with a member of the court line up so they can complain about their arrest. The right of "habeas corpus" is a human right that is only partially recognised in the European continental legal system. In contrast, in states with an Anglo-Saxon legal tradition, it belongs to the oldest and most elementary set of human rights.

When an alleged child murderer is caught, many do not understand why he is not tried and punished on the spot, even why he is not shot on the spot. The public usually wants to deny such a person every human right. An accused person, however, has the right to a fair trial. This is one of the important achievements of the modern *Rechtsstaat*. For a start, it is necessary to find out whether the alleged murderer actually committed the crimes of which he is accused. In the trial to determine this all parties have to be able to present their point of view.

The laws have to prevent the police being able arbitrarily to arrest disreputable people. After a serious crime the community rightfully is outraged and demands the immediate arrest of the guilty party. Understandably the police and the Office of Public Prosecutions want to move quickly in order to calm people down. In England as early the 17th century the so-called human right of "habeas corpus" was entrenched in what amounts to a constitutional document in order to stop the police being able to throw into jail every possible suspect unable to produce an alibi.

On the basis of this human right, which already was partly enshrined in the English Magna Carta of the 13th century, every person arrested by the police can demand to be presented immediately to a judge, to challenge the state's arbitrary restriction on his liberty. "Habeas corpus" applies to everyone taken into custody by the state, whether in the form of internment in a psychiatric clinic, military detention or legal guardianship. This right is at least partially incorporated into international human rights conventions as well as into the European human rights conventions.

Dictators and totalitarian governments instil fear in the population and political opponents because at any time, according to whim, they can throw people into jail. With the right to "habeas corpus" the all-pervading power of the state and its secret police can be broken. That is why the international community is trying, through the use of international guarantees, to place people under the protection of independent judges.

But when is a judge independent? To ensure that the judges of the Supreme Court are totally independent the American Constitution envisages appointment for life and guarantees that remuneration, once set, cannot be reduced. Thus the judges fear neither dismissal nor intimidation from a government that might threaten a salary cut. This constitutional guarantee of judicial independence belongs fundamentally to the human right of "habeas corpus".

To prevent the police from using leading questions to get incorrect admissions from people who have been detained, or from using torture to extract false confessions, the Supreme Court of the United States declared long ago in a trail-blazing judgment that people cannot be convicted of crimes if they were not informed of their rights upon arrest. The accused can refuse to say anything and is entitled immediately to contact a lawyer.

The highest court in America handed down this decision after it became clear that, in many States, dispro-portionate numbers of black people, but not whites, were being convicted of capital offences. This discrimination against a whole section of the population in criminal trials was only possible because the police could employ methods with the black minority that led to the false convictions of many in-nocent people.

Many, particularly members of the police and prosecutors, have protested against this liberal practice of the Supreme Court on the grounds that, ultimately, it leads to the guilty being set free, and that in many cases it makes it im-possible for the police to convict wrongdoers. This is truly one of the fundamental problems of human rights. Which should take precedence: the protection and safety of the population from violent crime, or the protection of the accused?

If the risk of violent crime is to be reduced to a minimum, freedoms have to be restricted enormously. Such restrictions on freedom automatically lead to an increase in the power of the police. If the expansion of police powers is not accompanied by improved scrutiny of the use of these powers, general experience tells us that there is danger that individual officers will succumb to the temptation to misuse their power against defenceless prisoners.

Here again we have to tread the fine line between the protection of the population on the one hand and human rights on the other. That is why in the international conventions it is explicitly envisaged that, in times of extreme danger, states can declare a state of emergency. In such a case human rights can at least partially be restricted. Only the prohibition on torture, that is, the human right to physical and emotional integrity, is not allowed to be restricted, even in a state of emergency.

Once a murderer is convicted the form of punishment and sentence also have to be judged in light of human rights. This raises the issue of the death penalty.

To date only an optional protocol to the European Human Rights Convention forbids the death penalty. However, in the light of human rights it is hard to justify the death penalty in times of peace.

Punishment fulfils different purposes: it is supposed to discourage other potential perpetrators from such crimes (deterrence), provide satisfaction for victims (revenge) and finally contribute to the re-integration of the criminal in society.

Those who commit a crime do not think that they will ever be caught. That is why the introduction of the death penalty does little to reduce crime. Capable police and efficient criminal prosecution contribute much more to the prevention of crime. Punishment of criminals can give satisfaction to victims. Without doubt, punishment also serves the aims of retribution, compensation and revenge. Whether the victims, however, get more satisfaction from the use of the death penalty than from a long prison sentence, with an opportunity for subsequent re-habilitation, seems doubtful in the majority of cases.

When it is at least doubtful that the use of the death penalty can satisfy this aim, it clearly is no longer justified from the standpoint of human rights. What gives the state and society the right to extinguish the life of a human being by state-sanctioned execution?

If people have committed capital crimes because they are psychologically ill or abnormal, the state must take steps to heal them. If they cannot be cured society has to protect itself from them. That is why all criminal codes provide for the incarceration of the incurably sick who are a danger to the community. The use of the death penalty against a psychologically ill person is, however, without a doubt an abuse of human rights. This is because people cannot be punished for acts committed under the influence of compulsive delusions.

With all other forms of criminal punishment the aim is re-integration into society. Perpetrators of crimes have to be able to live in society once more and to interact socially. This is indeed the most important aim of every form of criminal punishment. It also ultimately serves as an efficient form of prevention. That is because effective re-integration in society is the best way to minimise the dangerously high numbers of repeat-offenders.

17

Are Asylum-Seekers Humans?

For years a Yugoslavian family has been waiting for a ruling on their application for asylum in Switzerland. The father, who is married to a Croatian, does not want to fight against either the Croatians or against people from his own country. That is why he deserted first the Yugoslavian and then the Croatian armies. If he is deported he can expect to be convicted as a deserter in Serbia as well as in Croatia. The children already go to school in Switzerland and speak fluent German. Their father is trying to get over his depression by doing some casual work, and their mother carries the weight of the family with all its uncertainties plus the aggression of a hopeless husband.

Do these people belong to a lower class of humanity or are they human beings with a right to have their dignity respected? Do the children have a right to a school education like the Swiss children in their area? Does the family have a right to accommodation and social security like every other family? Does it have a private life that should be protected, or are officials allowed to enter the family home whenever they please, to get more details about their asylum application and the whereabouts of the family within Switzerland? Can these officials subject them to a body search during the course of a normal interview or take their money as a security deposit?

When asylum-seekers come to Switzerland they are first brought to a reception camp. There they receive a leaflet which, amongst other things, states the following:

"Your ... proof of identity must be surrendered ... While your application is being processed you are not allowed to return to your home country ... Your family members are not allowed to come to Switzerland until your application for asylum has been processed ... You are not allowed to leave the reception area without permission ... If you breach any of the duties of cooperation outlined here, you take the risk that your application for asylum will not be processed..."

What Swiss national would be prepared to accept this sort of harsh restriction on his freedom of movement, to hand over his identity papers, to submit to disciplinary measures without a judicial examination of the consequences which might result, namely the refusal to process an application for asylum?

People will object: "Ultimately no-one is obliged to enter Switzerland. After all, we Swiss cannot be responsible for the fact that war has broken out in the former Yugoslavia. We Swiss have to work hard too in order to survive. We cannot afford to have others sit back and relax as refugees and get paid for doing it. Anyway, our country is already overpopulated. We have accommodation problems of our own and have to make sure that we do not lose our jobs because employers are taking on asylum-seekers for low wages."

"Our schools are over-crowded with the children of foreign families. The education of our own children is therefore neglected. Are our own children, who have been living in Switzerland for years and whose parents have been paying taxes for years, supposed to sit at the same school desks as children of foreign cultures and races? Which human right is to take precedence: that of the Swiss or that of the refugee, for whose fate we are not responsible?"

These are the objections with which you are confronted when you take an interest in the fate of refugees.

Solutions can only be found if we understand that all human beings, of whatever religion, nationality or race, are equal. We are all humans with Reason, language, free will and the need for love, security and a home. When human beings come, for whatever reason, to our countries we bear responsibility for the protection of their human dignity.

All states are parts of a diversity of peoples that is moving towards a common destiny. The peace of the international community is indivisible and can, in the long term, only be preserved when not just states and peoples, but human beings as well are acknowledged as having equal value and equal rights.

All human beings are part of the international community to which our state also belongs. All human beings contribute to our ability to live and survive on our planet. States are not "islands of sovereignty" swinging freely in space. Human rights therefore bind all states in the same way.

Human rights, however, are the rights of the weak and the defenceless. Our first obligations are to them. That is why refugees who seek sanctuary in our country, as human beings with their own Reason and ability to make free decisions, have a valid claim to respect and protection.

18

The Right to Property

John Arup, a business man, has a large garden market in the suburbs of a city. Paul, the son of one of his employees, has already worked on Saturday afternoons in the garden for ages in order to earn some pocket money. Paul is paid $10 per hour. Two of his friends also want to earn some pocket money; so Paul asks Mr Arup if he can bring his friends along to work next Saturday and if they can also get paid for some gardening. Mr Arup agrees. However, he cannot offer more than $20 per hour for all three. How should he divide this amount between the three youngsters?

Paul is hard working and focused. But he tends to confuse the vegetable plots with a paddock, and he uses the scythe as if was felling trees!

Irmgard works somewhat slower, but is more careful and precise. She has a green thumb and knows how you are supposed to prune plants. She can even distinguish between weeds and flowers when they are all still shoots.

Stefan mostly day dreams. He lost his father long ago; now his mother is in hospital as well and he has to spend all his pocket money on his little sister who has not been given any toys in ages.

Who should earn more, who less? Mr Arup can divide the hourly wage according to three principles.

1. *Consideration of pre-existing rights:* Paul has already been working for a long time: he should not get a lower wage just because he brings his friends with him. Therefore he gets $10 and the remaining $10 must be shared by the two new-comers.

2. *Each according to merit:* In these circumstances Irmgard will be rewarded with the largest amount, the hard-working but clumsy Paul with a little less and the dreamy Stefan will have to be content with a wage packet that is almost empty.

3. *Each according to need:* If Mr Arup considers the needs of the three children then he will give dreamy Stefan, whose mother is in hospital, the most and the others a little less.

No principles for the distribution of property and income can be derived directly from human rights. States are largely free to find a system that best reflects their tradition, culture and living standards. Nevertheless, there are some important principles that, from the perspective of human rights, should be recognised in every system.

People who work hard do not want to live from hand to mouth forever; they want to save the proceeds for troubled times or to put it aside for their children. In the early days of the Middle Ages there was almost no opportunity for farmers to preserve the fruits of their labour for troubled times. The only possibility was to preserve the fruits in the basement for winter. The fruits that one could preserve the best were the nuts.

It was also with the nuts in the basement that the great political philosopher of the 17th century, John Locke, compared money. Money and capital are to a certain extent the fruits in the basement, which one can preserve and stockpile for much longer than nuts. With money you can buy and lease land, build and rent houses, purchase shares, invest, speculate or simply put savings in the bank, in order to profit from the interest on the account.

But people only have these opportunities when the "fruits" of their labour are secure; when the state cannot deprive them of the fruits of their labour through taxes, inflation or by way of confiscation. The right to use your property as you see fit, the right to live from the fruits of your labour, these are rights that also belong in the catalogue of human rights.

It is intrinsic to human dignity that the human being can work and live from the fruits of her labour, that she can put everything that she does not necessarily need to survive aside for her children or for later in her own life. If you deprive human beings of work, you deprive them of a fundamental part of their dignity. But work only has meaning for people when they ultimately live from their work. The right to work on the one hand and the right to property on the other have to be protected.

Does the human right to property also guarantee a particular economic system? Does the human right tell us which principle Mr Arup should use to distribute the wages amongst the three youngsters? There are no answers to this awkward question in the human rights conventions. In a liberal economic system the merits of labour will be assessed in the free market. This leads to a situation where everybody seeks success in the free market and therefore wants to provide the best "fruits" possible, that is, to use their labour optimally. This, however, is only possible, in the end, in an economic and corporate culture in which every competitor is respected.

In contrast, the merits of labour could be assessed by the state. In this case everybody will try to get as much influence over state politics as possible, in order to ensure that their labours are valued highly. It is obvious that in this system the power of the state bureaucracy will become immense. The state's accumulation of such power endangers human rights. Officials that make decisions on jobs, remuneration and product development possess authority that is almost uncontrollable. Practically nobody will be able to control these officials.

19

Freedom of Religion

In light of the continually increasing number of foreign children, our schools have to deal with the almost insoluble problem of acquainting children from a totally different culture with our way of life. In this process culture and religious conviction are often inseparable in practice. For example, many followers of the Islamic faith have the view that from a certain age onwards girls are not allowed to expose themselves to men. They are therefore required by the Koran to wear the chador. In this way, the girls' chador becomes an expression, indeed a symbol, of their religious convictions, just like the observance of Sunday mass for Catholics. These Muslims therefore invoke the human right to freedom of religion and conscience.

No doubt freedom of religion and conscience is one of the most important human rights. The relationship between an individual and his god, his religion and the hereafter touches the core of his soul. Nobody has the right to interfere with this core, to damage a person's convictions or even to attempt to change them.

The holy duty to spread religious truth and to ensure that people worship the *real* god belongs primarily to the various Christian denominations and to the Islamic faith. This belief in the missionary obligation, inherent in proselytising religions, has led to a situation in which a number of states that are guided by these religions deny the human right to freedom of religion and conscience.

That is why some Islamic states today still have major reservations about the Universal Declaration of Human Rights, in so far as it relates to the human right to religious freedom. In European countries the human right to freedom of religion and conscience developed out of a deep conflict within the Christian faith, that is, between Protestants and Catholics. Subjects were initially obliged to adopt the denomination of their ruler. In those days the members of opposing denominations at least received the right to emigrate to another country. It was only gradually that it became clear that the state should not intervene in religious affairs and that there can only be peace between the various religions when the state is neutral in matters of religion.

In the "school prayer" decision the Supreme Court of the United States decided that beginning the day with a prayer in public schools breaches state neutrality. The backlash against this decision shows that an acceptance of neutrality is not universally shared in the community. But if you take the human right to freedom of religion seriously, you have to acknowledge that in a pluralist society only a state that is neutral about religion can protect and respect the human right to freedom of religion and conscience for everyone to the same extent. Only in a state that is neutral towards religion can various religious communities live peacefully with one another, because they are ultimately all treated equally and no religious community will assume that state power can be misused for religious purposes.

In the 16th and 17th centuries many religious refugees left England to emigrate to America. When, during the foundation of the American State, freedom of religion was to be entrenched as a human right, some wanted to use the

Constitution to oblige the state to ensure that all religions were promoted and supported. After a long debate there was agreement on the opposite principle. The state should accordingly be absolutely neutral; it should not be able to support and promote any religion: "congress shall make no law respecting an establishment of religion, or prohibiting the free exercise thereof". Religion was thus declared in the American Constitution to be a private matter. Today there is no other country in which so many different religions can live as peacefully and closely with each other as in the United States.

In tradition-bound Europe, whose borders, after all, developed out of religious conflicts, other ways had to be found to guarantee freedom of religion. The pogroms of the 19th century and the Holocaust of the 20th century are evidence that the idea of an unreserved freedom of religion was foreign to many members of the Christian religion for a long time, and indeed in part has remained so. True freedom of religion can be realised only in a social climate where every faith is respected as part of human diversity and human dignity. Many societies, however, are far removed from this concept of tolerance.

The example of the chador in schools demonstrates this with great clarity. When a father forbade his daughter from attending compulsory school swimming lessons with boys, the education authorities took legal action to force the father to do so, even though he made it clear that the Koran forbids a Muslim woman from exposing herself to men. That is why he wanted to assert his human right to religious freedom, and that of his daughter, by appealing to the Federal Court against the decision of the authorities in the Canton of Zürich. The Federal Court recognised the human right in this particular situation and obliged the authorities to release the child from swimming lessons.

For many Swiss people this decision was incomprehensible. Surely it is the task of the school to ensure that children are integrated into society? If you want to live and work in our country you have to assimilate with our society. Naturally, you can still practise your religion in your private life. In school and in public, however, you have to abide by the country's customs and you cannot avoid integration by invoking the right to religious freedom. *A human right is not only a right of the minority, it is also a right of the majority*. The minority is not allowed to tyrannise the human right to freedom of religion and conscience. These and many other arguments could be heard when the decision of the Federal Court was discussed.

The very concept of human rights gives rise to their task of protecting minorities from majorities. Minorities have absolutely no chance of asserting their convictions politically against the political majority. Ultimately, they can protect themselves from unacceptable infringements of their rights only through the decision of a court.

It is self-evident that there are limits to religious freedom. A sect that preaches the end of the world cannot justify its poison gas attacks by invoking the right to freedom of religion. As with all other human rights, freedom of religion is limited by the rights of others.

Freedom of religion cannot be misused so as to endanger the health and the lives of other people. Exorcism, for example, is not to be protected, for it endangers the lives and mental integrity of other people. In individual cases it is often difficult to decide whether the teachings of a religious community should be protected or whether the public interest in health, life and public order justify a prohibition. Must a state, for example, allow female circumcision, which is demanded by some cultures and religions, or should it punish those responsible for inflicting bodily harm? Must a hospital acquiesce in the religious convictions of parents who are Christian Scientists and so refrain from operating on a seriously ill child that will not be able to survive without surgery?

There is no clear answer to such questions about the borders of life. It is essential, however, that such questions are not answered by the majority. It falls instead to the courts to decide in each case the extent to which an individual human right should have priority and be protected over the rights of the majority. The court will be guided in this by the conviction that the majority does not have the right to impinge on the religious freedom of the minority when no-one is endangered by their faith and an infringement of religious freedom would be an over-reaction.

20

Protection of Constitutional Rights

A few years ago the Swiss Government decreed that everyone travelling by car was required to wear a seat belt. Mr Spirig refused to do so and was fined by the police. He challenged the fine in the Federal Court. He thought that a person's freedom of movement, the right to decide for himself which risks to accept when travelling by car, belonged to the general human right of a person to have the opportunity for unimpeded development, and could therefore only be changed by law and not the government alone. In a notable decision, the Federal Court found in favour of Mr Spirig and held that a person's movement and development was part of his human freedom. This freedom could indeed be restricted by the state; but only the legislature, and not the government, could intrude on this freedom.

Why is the government not allowed to introduce regulations making the use of seat belts compulsory, when the legislature can? What is the difference between a rule made by the executive and a statute? Is it not splitting hairs for the Federal Court to quash the rulings of government, but refrain from questioning the rulings of the legislature?

Human rights can always be restricted up to a certain point. But it is fundamental that these restrictions are determined by the legislature rather than the executive. The executive has the task of administering the laws made by a democratically elected legislature. Without the specific authorisation of the legislature the executive may not restrict the freedom of citizens. A very important achievement of the modern state consists of ensuring that people are not at the mercy of the arbitrary whims of a government or bureaucracy. The rights of people can only be restricted by government or the bureaucracy if a statute that has been made by a democratically elected legislature explicitly allows this.

So human rights can be restricted where the democratic legislature, that is, the majority, agrees with these restrictions. Mind you, the majority of the parliament will have to think about whether it wants to unjustifiably curtail the rights of the people. This is because the parliamentary majority enacts laws under the scrutiny of the public, that is, the media. Everyone can see which parliamentarian supports restrictions on the rights of car drivers and passengers.

The parliamentarians themselves do not want to enact laws against the will of their voters, as they have their re-election to think of. At the end of the parliamentary term they have to account to the electorate for what they did with their mandate. In Switzerland, citizens even have the right to call a referendum on laws with which they do not agree. Laws which do not have a clear justification for restricting the freedom of a large majority of citizens therefore do not stand a chance to survive the challenge of a referendum. Democracy and human rights are thus strongly intertwined.

The requirement that seat belts be worn, for example, can be justified. It can be proved that wearing a seat belt leads to fewer injuries arising from accidents, which in turn affects the cost of car and disability insurance. The general public should not have to bear costs incurred by dare-devil drivers. If the state builds streets and freeways with tax-payers' money then it should also be able to enact rules which reduce the risk of serious injury.

With such considerations one would not, however, be able to enact a general prohibition on swimming, in order to reduce the risk of accidents and the related costs to the general public. Skiing and swimming are important forms of relaxation and therefore important to the fundamental freedom of the individual. That is why such prohibitions can only be enacted in exceptional circumstances, as when skiers are banned from using particularly dangerous slopes that are prone to avalanches or when the state requires that scuba-divers have a licence.

Obviously it would never occur to a legislature to institute a general ban on swimming. Nevertheless, even a democratic legislature can sometimes infringe the human rights of minorities. For human rights are not just a barrier protecting the majority from despotic government, they are also a shield for the minority against the majority of the legislature. The Australian Constitution of 1900, for example, provided that indigenous Australians should not be counted for electoral purposes. They were also denied the vote by legislation. The Australian Constitution still recognises the possibility that state legislatures might deny the vote to state residents on the ground of their race, although, fortunately, this does not happen in fact. Here a majority of the actual founders of the Constitution had restricted the human right to participate in political affairs.

What is the position today with laws which curtail the rights of ethnic or linguistic minorities? Can, for example, a community that speaks one language require a minority language group to use that language too? This would be analogous to the demands of the legislature in Quebec on English speakers within the French speaking region, and those of the Flemish legislature in Belgium on francophone Walloons in respect of the Dutch language region.

According to international conventions for the protection of human rights, the majority of a legislature may only restrict freedom when this is necessary in the interests of the general public, for example, for the protection of life, limb and health.

The majority is not affected by such infringements; on the contrary, it is interested in restricting the rights of minorities. There is thus a need for another institution with the task of protecting the powerless minority through those human rights which are elementary to them. This task is currently undertaken in many countries by constitutional courts. In the interest of the minority, these constitutional courts have to be able to bind the democratically elected legislature.

Constitutional courts, however, are not always in agreement. For instance, the American Supreme Court for a long period placed the right of a woman to make her own decisions about her pregnancy before the right to life of the child. In contrast the German Federal Constitutional Court decided that, together with the right of the woman, the right of the developing child to life had to be taken into account. This right was only allowed to be restricted in particular cases.

These controversial opinions show us only that the question of human rights in borderline cases remains controversial and always will. Borderline cases are no reason to doubt human rights. Thanks to the institution of the constitutional court, many fundamental social conflicts and disagreements between state and citizen have been able to be solved. The increase in the jurisdiction of constitutional courts since the

Second World War shows that states are more and more convinced that *without the protection of constitutional rights there can be next to no protection of the human rights of minorities.* This is one of the reasons why international courts of human rights receive increasing authority to protect those minorities from the majority where they receive no protection through their own existing institutions.

21

The Rule of Law

Anyone who reads the diary of Anne Frank can conceive what it must be like to live hidden from public view in a small sealed room, always fearing that one will be deported to a concentration camp. Every morning the re-occurring nightmares come to an end, every knock on the door triggers panic attacks and every ring of the phone makes one start with fright. One of the worst characteristics of totalitarian states is that they authorise the police to enter homes at any time and search them for alleged terrorists or enemies of the state.

Can someone who has never lived under a dictatorship understand the fear with which people live day after day, understand the shock that ripples through their limbs every time the door bell rings? Is it possible to describe how the throats of persecuted victims choke with fear when they hear of another round of deportations from their quarter? Paralysed, they are condemned to wait until they too experience the final tightening of the noose.

A state which allows officials and police to arbitrarily force their way into homes in order to arrest and remove people they find there is a state that is both authoritarian and contemptuous of Mankind. In a state under the rule of law the police can force their way into a home only if they have a legal search warrant. A person can be arrested only if a judge has issued a warrant for that person's arrest.

An arrest-warrant can be issued only where the legal requirements for an arrest have been fulfilled. This will undoubtedly not be the case with troublesome political opponents who are not guilty of a crime. Criminal codes with vague and uncertain definitions of crimes, which can be used by the authorities to brand every critic an enemy of the state or the constitutional order and lock him behind bars, are contrary to the rule of law and violate human rights to legal certainty and freedom of expression.

When people are dragged from their homes in the dead of night they are usually deported to secret locations. There they are cut off from the environment without any opportunity to make contact with the outside world. Even family members know nothing about the fate of their mother, father, husband, brother, sister. For "incommunicados" their most elementary human rights require that they know that they have been registered and that independent institutions know of their incarceration.

Totalitarian states do not allow forms of review which could protect people from such abuses. It is usually only international organisations that can, at least in certain cases, provide prisoners with some form of protection. One of these organisations is the International Committee of the Red Cross ("the ICRC"). The ICRC can rely on the Geneva Conventions, which have been ratified by the states, and which gives it a mandate under international law to provide limited protection to political prisoners in states where there is internal unrest. It can register prisoners and provide lists of those prisoners; it can also organise written correspondence and ensure regular visits by members of the Red Cross.

Unfortunately the ICRC is only very rarely allowed access to prisoners by the authorities, so in many cases it has to stand by and watch how authoritarian dictators marginalise the political opposition.

Now and then the authorities are interested in having the ICRC on side. They want to use the visiting rights of the ICRC to make known to the world that they are abiding by international human rights standards. The ICRC traditionally only provides reports about their prisoner visits, and particularly about acts of torture, where applicable, to authorities of the country in question, rather than the public in general. The authorities thus risk little by complying with the ICRC. As, however, there are always officials in dictatorships that want to prevent the worst abuses of human rights, such reports are unlikely to be totally ineffective. Thus a former Justice Minister of such a country affirmed that it was only thanks to these reports that he was able to control his own department and bring his subordinates to account.

In order to prevent the misuse of the ICRC as an instrument of propaganda, it visits prisoners only when three conditions are satisfied: first, the ICRC has to be able to see all prisoners; secondly, it has to have unhindered access to prisoners at all times and, thirdly, it has to be able to speak with prisoners without the presence of any third person.

Amnesty International operates very differently. This organisation listens systematically to reports of escapees or released prisoners, in order to get the most comprehensive and objective view possible of the situation in that country. These statements and the opinion of Amnesty International are then published. In this way states can be accused before the spotlight of international public opinion.

The discussion of human rights abuses before the spotlight of international opinion admittedly is a two-edged sword. Often this path subjects human rights abuses to the huge whirlpool of international politics. They lose their credibility as well as their international importance. Politicians armed with media reports, who denounce the human rights abuses of other states, usually do this less to help the victims than to pay homage to public opinion in their own country. When human rights abuses are no longer at the centre of international politics these politicians are no longer worried about the fate of the victims.

Every action that is designed primarily to help the victims can be successful only if intervention is discrete. It is important not to give the authorities the impression that the primary aim of the action is to discredit them politically. A government should not have to fear that an international commitment to human rights could be exploited by the opposition and that it might serve to undermine its national and international credibility. As soon as human rights become strategic weapons to topple troublesome governments, the real victims have little chance of having their suffering alleviated.

Those who are particularly at risk live in countries where the authorities pretend not to tolerate human rights abuses, yet at the same time they tolerate or even support the mass media, private organisations and death squads, which hound minorities and act as the governments' thugs in threatening, kidnapping, torturing and murdering people.

States and governments cannot be content merely to equip courts with the necessary authority to condemn human rights violations. *Governments that take human rights seriously must actively employ the police and the administration to protect defenceless citizens and minorities from abuses by the majority.* Information campaigns and the school system need to be placed at the service of human rights, so that the necessary understanding for the respect of minorities, outsiders and foreigners can grow.

The international community tries continually to create new institutions with which human rights abuses can effectively be prevented. Inspections by the United Nations, Observers and Special Envoys for the Protection of Minorities sent by the Organisation for Security and Cooperation in Europe are but a few examples demonstrating the despairing search for institutions, procedural guarantees and methods to save the increasingly undermined institution of the rule of law.

22

In the Grasp of the State Administration

Mr Braithwaite works in the state administration. His wife is Russian. That is why he spent a lot of time over the past thirty years with his family in the Soviet Union. Every trip to the East was registered by the police so that they could notify the relevant agencies of the risks posed by Braithwaite.

Martin Stucki is a student who is working on his dissertation on Marxist philosophy. For this reason he frequently consults books about communism in the national library. This level of interest in communist literature is suspicious and has to be registered with the police.

The great fear of communist machinations led the police in Australia, as in many other states, to create files on those who did not behave conventionally. This close surveillance caused great consternation. It is, however, what happens when an administration can set its own tasks and work largely without supervision.

When the human right to protection of the private sphere is not taken seriously the big brother state can spy on the population's most intimate sphere of activity.

The state acts through its officials. The man next door is a policeman, and so he may have access to information about me. The mother of a class-mate and friend of my children works with the police and could possibly harm our family through the use of such information. We are all at the mercy of officials who profess to spy in the name of the national interest on the peoples' private sphere.

The protection of elementary human rights begins with the right to a private sphere free from state interference. The private sphere is endangered not only in dictatorships. It is unprotected in the era of electronic information technology in modern industrial states as well.

How can you protect yourself from a police-force which, entirely on its own authority and in the alleged national interest, has the nerve to spy on respectable citizens? What has to be done to prevent information gathered by all levels of government through their respective bureaucracies and agencies, such as the hospitals, schools, universities, social in-surance organisations etc, being one day summarised in an all encompassing database that would reveal the most personal of information to those entitled to use it?

We are already at the mercy of bureaucracies that network public databases with one another and that have at their disposal the complete range of documents on file with state departments.

That is why a way has to be found to prevent inscrutable "administrations" from eroding the freedom of the individual through their all-encompassing webs of information. The right to privacy is a human right that cannot be guaranteed by judges alone.

That is why laws have to empower particular statutory bodies to ensure, on their own initiative, that public officials not only do not abuse their authority, but also exercise it cautiously with the required respect for the private sphere of citizens. Such statutory bodies, which have a high degree of freedom to keep watch on the administration in the interests of citizens, were introduced more than 200 years ago in Sweden in the form of so-called "ombudsmen".

The "ombudsman" in Sweden is appointed by parliament and has the job of examining the complaints of citizens against the administration. He can only do his job in a way that produces confidence if he can independently assess all complaints, and can, of his own initiative, scrutinise all acts of the administration.

The human right to the protection of privacy cannot be asserted effectively through judicial supervision. Citizens, the usual plaintiffs, are in no position to assess what types of information the administration keeps and how this information is used. The scale of today's administration, the complexities and impenetrability of the apparatus of state, mean that people are at the mercy of the state in a way they find frightening.

They are consequently suspicious and are afraid of "Big Brother". They shy away from defending themselves for fear of retaliation of some kind. That is why there is a need for additional institutions which, with understanding and tact, seek dialogue between administration and citizen and which can re-establish confidence in an anonymous bureaucracy.

Politicians often want to give ombudsmen only a sort of alibi function, in order to "demonstrate" their own willingness to be subject to scrutiny, rather than giving them the necessary authority to do their job well. The Swedish ombudsman, by contrast, can examine everything, including the most secret activities of the administration. She can decide what to gather information about. She can take action in response to a complaint or on her own initiative. If she comes to the conclusion that the administration has to change its practice or has behaved improperly, she can, where necessary, institute legal proceedings or reprimand the administration in a report to parliament. In every case she is at least entitled to make suggestions to the administration about ways they could improve their credibility.

23

Human Rights in Social Life

Bans on smoking in restaurants, in aeroplanes and in workplaces have brought smokers into the arena of human rights. They are of the opinion that bans on smoking restrict their human rights. Non-smokers, on the other hand, seek bans on smoking because they claim that passive smoking damages their health. They invoke the right to life.

Are you allowed to invoke one right in order to restrict the human rights of others? It is at least clear that members of the Christian faith cannot invoke the right to freedom of religion to set fire to mosques. A bank has just as little excuse for demanding that its employees follow a particular religious faith.

But can the director of a bank dismiss employees because they did not want to join his political party? Can he expect them to subscribe to a newspaper that closely reflects his point of view? Can a large company place hidden cameras in the office that are used to monitor the working habits of employees?

All these questions touch on controversial human rights issues. Human rights are primarily there to protect citizens from interference by the state. For in a state under the so-called rule of law only the state can order the use of force. No company is allowed to use force to compel its employees to take certain actions. The state alone has the so-called monopoly on force. That is why officials that can exercise force have to be watched particularly carefully.

But you can frighten people without resort to force and coercion. Financial dependence, for example, can in practice just as surely lead to slavery as can fear of police terror. Should human rights be observed by public authorities, yet play no role at all in the regulation of relations between people?

Even the largest bank is dependent on the state legal system when it wants to solve an industrial dispute with its employees. If an employee is dismissed he can contest the dismissal in court. Without judicial dispute resolution peaceful relations between people are scarcely possible. Sometimes even those who do not work for a company or organisation are dependent on the use of force, such as incarceration of the guilty or police protection.

The state, however, can only resort to the use of force when this does not undermine the human rights of third parties. Without doubt the state police cannot be used to enforce inhuman forms of discrimination, such as that expressed in the sign "Turks are not permitted to enter this restaurant". In contrast, the sign "Smoking is not permitted in this restaurant" can indeed be enforced through the state sanctioned use of force when a group of smokers threatens to fill the room with smoke. But no-one has the right to discriminate against a particular group because of their race, religion or nationality.

The manager of the restaurant cannot invoke the human right to the free enjoyment of property or to freedom to trade. His restaurant can only function if it is open to the public. He is not allowed to restrict access to a particular, in this case non-Turkish, clientele.

No-one's health is threatened when Turks sit in the restaurant. The non-smokers, by contrast, feel that their health is endangered when they have to sit with smokers in the same restaurant. So long as no-one is bothered or disturbed, everyone has the right to behave as they want. When, however, it objectively can be demonstrated that the health or well-being of others is threatened, the human right to freedom of personal development can be restricted. This includes smoking.

These examples also show that the distinction between permissible discrimination against smokers and impermissible discrimination against a particular group of people, which amounts to contempt for Mankind, is not easy to apply to individual cases. In a free market, for example, employees who have been dismissed may be able to work for competitors. Similarly, tenants can move if the owner of the home in which they are living monitors the rooms with hidden cameras.

Many conflicts can indeed be solved without state regulation. There are, however, cases in which someone's dependence on a private company is almost as strong as that on the state, or in which discrimination is so extreme that the state has to protect the troubled minority. In these cases *human rights not only offer protection from interference by the state, but also from the conduct, contemptible to Mankind, of third parties*, whose discriminatory measures are ultimately only possible within the framework of a state that protects them.

24

On Equality Before the Law and Its Limits

People are equal and therefore to be treated equally. Are the laws of a state nevertheless allowed to distinguish between various "categories" of people? Only someone with a teaching certificate can become a teacher; only someone who has passed the driving test is allowed to drive a car. There is nothing wrong with this; but what about the following cases: only those who can afford a heart transplantation should be healed when suffering from heart disease; only men should be allowed to drive trains; women do not have to do military service; girls have to knit at school, while the boys are allowed to do handicraft; adolescents are a greater risk, so they have to pay higher car insurance premiums.

The human right to equality before the law forms the basis of every legal system. Only those who recognise that people are fundamentally equal will fight against the enslavement, against apartheid and the extermination of entire human races. Those who on the other hand take the view that there are fundamental differences between people, that there are for example races that are more intelligent than others, will justify the oppression of "subhumans" and fight for the award of privileges to the "master race".

The principle of equality before the law of all Mankind is uncontroversial. What is difficult, however, is its application to a concrete case. Sometimes you are not allowed to make a distinction between people, but on other occasions people have to be treated differently. Like is to be treated alike, the different to be treated differently. All human beings are endowed with Reason, so all human beings must be treated equally. So why should the young work, but not the old? Obviously like should only be treated alike and the different treated differently where this can objectively be justified. Children have to go to school, but adults do not. This inequality is justified because it is necessary. But when is unequal treatment necessary?

For a long time it was accepted that women are paid less money by employers because they, in general, do not spend as much time at work as men (earlier retirement, absence during child rearing, etc), because women do not have the same function as men in society or even because they were not seen to have the same abilities as men. Today this unequal treatment is no longer justified. For the existing socially unequal division of roles between men and women, according to the current point of view, no longer justifies political or legal unequal treatment of the sexes.

Even if many women still have the primary child rearing role in the family, this does not entitle the state to rely on the differences in the division of roles when, for example, discriminating against women in the provision of social security and in the law of marriage. The division of roles between the sexes within society is thus, according to the view held in Western states, not an objectively justifiable ground for statutory unequal treatment.

Unequal treatment therefore is only justified where a social consensus accepts a relevant inequality between people which requires unequal treatment. Adolescents under the age of 18 can thus be denied the right to vote; women, who are not under-represented in the public service, in contrast, according to a recent decision of European Court of Human Rights, are, as a matter of principle, not to be employed on a preferential basis.

But what is the position with respect to foreigners? The argument that foreigners should be denied the right to vote is clear enough. Every member of the nation is entitled to take part in the election. If you belong to "the People", you are a member of the sovereign. Foreigners, however, are major contributors to the national income. Many are well acquainted with public institutions and speak the native language fluently. On the basis of these considerations the Scandinavian states, as a matter of principle, guarantee all foreigners the right to vote, at least in local elections. Ultimately we have to seriously ask ourselves if a democracy can still be a real democracy where the 10-20% of the population who are foreigners, to which a country gives shelter, are denied the right to vote and stand for public office.

25

Freedom of Expression

In 1983, just after the military campaigns in Lebanon that were subject to massive criticism in Israel, the peace movement "Peace Now" in Jerusalem called for a demonstration for peace in the besieged state of Israel. A country at war, with fragile lulls in the fighting along its borders, permitted demonstrations calling for a final peace to be made with an irreconcilable enemy. A country with extremist settlers on the one side, who long for "Greater Israel", and the Palestinians on the other, who deny the small state the right to exist on "their" Islamic-Arabic territory; it is this country that allows the public expression of opinion, even though the majority feels that this endangers the very existence of their country, and refuses to use the police to silence a peace movement that opposes government policy.

More than 100,000 citizens were able, through a peaceful demonstration, to express their opinion and demonstrate their indignation at the current ruling majority. What other small country would have permitted such a demonstration that so clearly opposed the government in this tense situation? The human right to freedom of expression was more important that the risk of disturbing the public order.

The human right to freedom of expression is the hope of the minority through dialogue to convince the majority of the correctness of its view. Freedom of expression belongs to the fundamental core of the intellectual existence of human beings. Man, as a being endowed with Reason, can only exist when he himself can make up his own mind and act according to his convictions.

Freedom of conscience is the primal right of every human being. But what use is the freedom of secret thoughts when you are not allowed to voice them? No person is an island. People can only exist in a society with other human beings. The opportunity to discuss your opinions with others and to share them with friends is fundamental to human experience.

Now one must accept, just as with other human rights, that freedom of expression is subject to certain limits. Nobody, for instance, has the right during a rock concert in an overcrowded concert hall to suddenly scream "fire" without cause. Panic would be unavoidable, and nobody knows how many people would be injured or crushed to death.

The right to express an opinion cannot be allowed directly to endanger other human beings. But where do you draw the line? Lenin, for instance, thought that only communists had freedom of expression. In many democracies people think that freedom of expression cannot apply to those who reject tolerance and want to change the system of government by force.

It is on this basis, for instance, that parties with radical policies and extremist demands are forbidden in Germany. Anyone who demands unacceptable changes to the constitution is considered a radical and cannot get work as an official in the public service or be elected as a member of the German Parliament. Years ago a train driver, for example, was dismissed from public service because he was a member of the communist party.

The Turkish state organised its constitution along those same lines. In Turkey, state unity and legal equality are of the utmost importance. People who question state unity by, for example, demanding autonomy for the Kurds, are labelled radicals because their aim is unconstitutional.

In the United States in the fifties an unprecedented witch-hunt began against suspected communists. Anyone who could be accused of having "un-American" opinions was persecuted as a communist. This lasted until the American Supreme Court stated that as a matter of principle, as long as there is "no clear and present danger" to state and society, all expression of opinion is allowed.

In times of direct threat to the existence of the state, on the other hand, certain opinions will be banned from public discussion. For example, in Switzerland during the Second World War parties that "endangered the state" were banned. One controversial regulation remains from that time. It requires every political statement by a foreigner in public to be approved.

In England, by contrast, freedom of expression and freedom of the press were never restricted, despite the great threat during the Second World War and even during the bombing of London. But after the attack on Pearl Harbour the American Supreme Court, in a serious of highly controversial decisions, justified and consequently declared permissible in light of the emergency discriminatory measures against Americans of Japanese origin.

So in real life the extent to which freedom of expression is protected depends on tolerance and internal strength, stability and self-confidence in democracy and society. Nevertheless, it should not be the government's job to say which opinions are permissible. A constitutional court alone should be allowed to draw the line between the impermissibly dangerous and the merely unpalatable opinion which can be expressed.

In doing this, courts must take into account that they have no power behind them other than Reason. It is only by taking small steps that they can guide the majority and protect struggling minorities. Radical judgments, vehemently opposed by the great majority, can undermine the legitimacy of the court and thus do long-term damage to the institution of judicial review itself.

26

Freedom of the Press

Anti-racism laws in Switzerland prohibit and penalise statements which deny that millions of Jews were gassed in the concentration camp of Auschwitz. A claim that these laws infringed the freedom of the press led to a referendum aimed at overturning them. In a shocking advertising campaign, the Benetton fashion house promoted its products with the image of a bloodied uniform of a soldier tortured during an actual war. Had Benetton infringed the freedom of the press? A while ago in Germany a pamphlet was published which provocatively used the statement of a German poet, *Soldiers are murderers*, and aroused indignation and repulsion. Many have attributed the depression of the late Princess of Wales to the unjustified intrusion by the media into her private life. In 1995, a student newspaper published in Melbourne included an article on "The Art of Shoplifting". Should the publication be banned, because it promotes shoplifting, or is it merely a provocative attempt by students to question the sanctity of private property?

Television images, which in the seventies brought the horrors and atrocities of the Vietnam war into every American lounge room, made a fundamental contribution to the change in public opinion about the Vietnam war in the United States. Today, the images of CNN report the horrors of the war in

Yugoslavia and have a fundamental influence on international politics. No doubt this horrible civil war was fuelled by the hate campaign of the media.

Should all publications be protected in the name of freedom of the press? The invention of the printing press by Gutenberg was critical to Luther's ability to make his Ninety-Five Theses known to the public at large after he nailed them to the church, and hence to initiate the Reformation.

Freedom of the press is a most effective instrument of democracy with which to keep the authorities in check. That is why the flag of human rights has been held so high for so long. However, the authorities realised long ago that they can instrumentalise the press for their own interests as well.

The battle of the Italians against the press monopoly of Berlusconi, the media magnate, demonstrates all too clearly how freedom can be misused. The powerful exploit the freedom of the press to create media monopolies, with which they undermine the foundation of that freedom, namely, competition between opinions. There is little that can be done to fight this giant democratically. Through a press monopoly, citizens can be manipulated to such an extent that they approve of the very source which makes up their minds for them.

Freedom of the press can only fulfil its function as a check on power when the differing points of view within the community can compete with each other. If the press only publishes one point of view and especially if this point of view itself is "fabricated", the press deprives this human right of value.

Anglo-Saxon countries have always afforded freedom of the press the highest priority. They accept almost all risks, simply to prevent governments being able to decree which opinions can be presented to citizens. The slander of politicians, the televising of murder trials, the total exposure of the private lives of individual people, advertisements for law firms specialising in divorces, the stage-managing of the landing of American troops on the coast of Somalia just for television: everything is justified in the name of the human right to freedom of the press.

On the European continent the limits are reached much more quickly. The state, for instance, is allowed to prohibit the dissemination of the so called Auschwitz-lie. The Holocaust has such a deep, even religious, significance for Jewish people that the denial of Auschwitz becomes an attack on their religion. For many, Auschwitz made visible in the most terrible way so far the torment to which the Jewish people have been subjected. That is why the spreading of the Auschwitz-lie is not only the spreading of an untruth; at the same time it ridicules the symbol of the suffering of a people as well.

Not every Benetton advertisement is protected by the European version of freedom of the press. There is no direct television coverage of murder trials. Furthermore, when the press write articles, state laws allow those affected to publish a reply if they think that the article is wrong.

There is no truth which governments can simply prescribe. They can only gain acceptance through conflicting opinion. People have to decide which view they find the more convincing. Truth cannot be decreed; truth has to gradually gain acceptance through more convincing arguments, circulated freely, so that the better argument can prove itself against conflicting arguments. Those who do not want dictatorship have to accept the risk that freedom of the press will be misused.

But who can guarantee that in a conflict between opinions the right one ultimately will come out in front? To accept this you must accept that human beings are capable of distinguishing between right and wrong because of their rationality. An individual in a society surrounded by conflicting opinion is a "sovereign" being who must make an autonomous decision about what is right and wrong.

There have always been nations that have plunged into war and other atrocities by letting themselves be seduced by unjustifiable opinions. So why should a policy of social and historical openness mean that what is right for humanity will gain acceptance over the long term? Because historical experience shows that the truth as declared by a dictator generates far more misery than the temporary chaos of a democracy misled by inaccurate media reports.

For nearly 2000 years the philosophy of the Stoics has taught that there has to be an invisible order, an invisible hand, that ensures that in unimpeded competition between opinions and points of view the right one ultimately will gain acceptance. Exactly as in nature where, despite apparent chaos, order triumphs, in the unimpeded competition of ideas and opinions the right one will triumph. Those who fight for an unrestricted freedom of the press have no guarantee that truth will eventually emerge, but history shows that is it likely to do so.

27

Human Rights for the Unemployed, Homeless and Beggars

What good is freedom of the press and freedom of expression if practically no-one can read? What is the point of freedom of religion and conscience if religious communities cannot afford priests? Why should the private sphere of the home be protected if only a few can afford magnificent palaces and much of the rest of the population barely finds shelter? How can we worry about human dignity if the poor survive only from the rubbish of the rich? How can one affirm the unimpeded development of the individual when in one place people have too much work and in another they are unemployed? For freedom to become a reality, the pre-conditions for the exercise of human rights must be created so that people can actually make use of their rights.

Human dignity and freedom can exist only when rights which protect an individual's liberty are supplemented by social rights, that is, so called second generation rights, such as the right to a job, the right to an education, the right to a home, and so on.

But how can the right to a job or the right to a home be enforced? If the government prohibits the publication of a newspaper article, the publisher can use the right to freedom of the press to get the prohibition overturned by a court. The court does not have to force the government to take particular measures in order for the right to be asserted.

But when people are homeless and the government does not give them a home, how can a court enforce their right? A court has no money at its disposal to build houses or rent flats; it cannot force the owner of a flat to evict a family with two flats from the second one, or require the owner to take a second family into their own small flat. In such situations one person's right to a home would infringe the right to unimpeded development and the property rights of others. But which right should be given priority here? Because social rights cannot easily be protected by judges, there is a temptation to throw the baby out with the bathwater and deny that these are human rights at all. Rights which cannot be asserted by judges, it is claimed, ultimately are not rights at all.

Most recent developments, however, particularly in the European Union, demonstrate that the contribution of courts may not be so limited, and that the authority of judges may have been interpreted too narrowly until now. The European Court, for instance, recently required Italy to pay compensation because it had not complied promptly with its obligation under European Union law to expand social security for the unemployed.

The capacity of courts to maintain a subtle balancing of human rights, social harmony and needs of the public purse has convincingly been shown by previous interpretations of rights designed to protect an individual's liberty. Why is it not possible for courts in the area of second-generation human rights to take into account the social plight of individual people on the one hand while bearing in mind the interests of the state on the other?

Human rights are the rights of all human beings. Above all, they give minorities the opportunity to defend their human dignity through the courts. Pure majority rule can lead to minorities being inhumanly disadvantaged. Ultimately, minorities can only protect themselves through the courts. So if human rights are to be taken seriously, legal protection cannot be limited to rights to freedom. Legal protection necessarily has to encompass social rights.

What is the difference between heaven and hell? Chinese Buddhists give the following profound reply, which everyone concerned with human rights should take to heart:

In hell starving skeletons sit at tables on which the most delicious of dishes are served. The dinner companions, however, cannot enjoy the food because the chopsticks, as soon as the companions pick them up, grow longer than their limbs, so that they cannot use them. But those who in live in heaven sit at the same tables with the same chopsticks, yet are well fed; for they use the long chopsticks to pass food to one another.

28

Once Again: Legal Equality and Equality of Opportunity

In the fifties, the majority of blacks in the United States used all available means to fight discrimination against their children in schools. In those days, in almost all areas of public life and society, particularly in the Southern States, racial segregation, that is, apartheid, was regarded as the holiest principle of legal equality. Schools, restaurants, railway carriages, even toilets were designated either for the exclusive use of whites or the exclusive use of blacks. In the interests of "legal equality" it was carefully ensured that both races were treated equally, yet separate from each other.

Forty years ago the Brown family instituted proceedings in the Supreme Court against the politics of apartheid in schools. In particular, they drew attention to the fact that educating black children separately from whites led to severe discrimination. The principle "equal, but separate" did not reflect the principle of "legal equality" because the minority saw it as discrimination. It was discriminatory because black children had to learn in schools in which only children whose parents themselves had received poor schooling were educated. The inequality of opportunity for blacks, due to the principle of apartheid in the schools, was said to be degrading and to violate the human dignity of the black minority.

In a thought provoking decision in 1954, the Supreme Court decided for the first time in favour of the black minority. It took the view that in order to decide whether part of the community was being treated unequally by the law, it had to work out whether treatment which appeared to be equal had discriminatory effects. The minority in practice was discriminated against by the system of segregated schools, because there were far less educational opportunities for them in these schools. Segregated school education was perceived by the minority as degrading discrimination and the right to legal equality was infringed.

The court began with the assumption that, as a matter of principle, all people are equal. Apartheid therefore is a clear breach of the elementary human right to legal equality.

This decision signalled an unparalleled movement towards the practical equality of the black minority in the United States.

But, afterwards, people began to realise that it was not enough to merely require schools to accept black children. The white population had increasingly cut itself off in particular suburbs from the black population, and used exclusive suburban schools. The effect was to create purely white schools once again because the black minority had to live in poor suburbs, far away from the white suburbs.

Once against the Supreme Court intervened. This time it decided that the state had to do more than passively ensure that black children could attend the schools. The state, as well as private schools subsidised by the state, had to ensure through positive measures that schools were mixed with white and black children.

But the black minority still maintained that they were discriminated against in higher education. For selection based purely on achievement meant that proportionally far less black people than whites had the opportunity to study at good universities. The black minority, as a result of discrimination over the centuries and cultural differences, could not compete with the white majority. The criteria for determining "high achievers" also reflected white culture. And so they demanded that every institution of higher education be required to accept a certain number of black applicants, reflecting a quota created for the minority, despite a record of lesser achievement.

These measures, which ultimately privilege a certain minority, treating people *unequally* so that the minority can catch up with the majority, are described as "affirmative action" in the United States. They have spread to all areas of state and society.

Today, these measures are controversial once again. Some white people express the opinion that positive discrimination treats the white population unequally. Relying on the principle of legal equality, they demand a return to *formal* equality so that all human beings, regardless of actual differences, are treated in a manner that formally is equal. Accordingly, in a recent decision, the Supreme Court declared that it is inconsistent with legal equality for a state to ignore geographic considerations when determining electoral boundaries, and instead to draw them in such a way that sufficient black people can be represented in the legislature.

The effect of positive discrimination once again is to distinguish between people who are equal in other respects but who have different coloured skin. The principle of the American "melting pot" does not allow discrimination of this kind.

The European Court also recently decided that affirmative action in favour of women by the city of Bremen, because they were under-represented in the city administration, breached the principle of legal equality.

The example of the black minority in the United States shows *how difficult it is for the principle of legal equality, and indeed human rights in general, to be asserted through legal measures.* How can a law counter discrimination that is embedded in the culture of a society? Inter-mixing in a society cannot be achieved unless it is actually accepted by a broad majority of the population.

We need to accept that the effective implementation of legal equality, like the realisation of true equality of opportunity, will require many years, even decades. If you try to do too much too quickly you will encounter a strong backlash.

The "melting pot" principle, which assumes that people are fundamentally equal and requires the state to do everything to enable races and cultures to mix, today belongs to a set of core principles for the protection of minorities in American politics.

The principle may be suitable for a country of immigrants that was originally open to many peoples, and had to ensure that the people of different cultures could live in one country peacefully with each other. To what extent black people, in their collective consciousness, count themselves amongst these immigrants may be open to question. Finally, we have to realise that the politics of the "melting pot" was possible only because the indigenous population, the Indians, paid a bloody price for it. Today they still live as a tiny minority in reserves, territorially separate from the "melting pot", because they do not want to be integrated into this open society.

In the end the "melting pot" principle was dependent on equal language education for all. But as soon as the language question becomes a human rights question, territory and borders between one linguistic region and the other also become decisive factors in the legal and practical division between majorities and minorities.

29

The Right to a Healthy Environment

From an ecological perspective human history can be divided into three long periods: the period of the nature-obeyer, the period of the nature-dominator and the period of the nature-partner. Initially humans had to learn to live and survive under the reign of nature. Nature ruled the human with divine authority. It was the time of the animist nature religions, in which the powers of nature were attributed to the divine. As humans through fire gradually succeeded in taming the reign of nature, we began to dominate nature. "Make the earth subservient to you" was the motto of the nature-dominator. With an understanding of the laws of nature, human beings were able gradually to conquer the forces of nature.

Nature, however, cannot be subordinated. While we know individual laws of nature, we are far from knowing what effects intrusions into nature will have on the entire ecosystem. As nature-dominators, we overlooked the fact that we also are part of nature and that we cannot work against nature, only with it and for it. The nature-dominator thus has gradually had to change into a nature-partner.

Are we humans allowed, in the interests of our personal and economic development, an unrestricted right, for example, to pollute the air with the exhaust from our cars and heating systems or to destroy the lungs of the earth through the clearing of forests? Human rights are limited rights. The present generation has no right to undermine the survival of humankind or the quality of life of the next generation through the exploitative destruction of the environment.

What would the present generation honestly think if we had to deal with environmental dangers that were created by people more than a thousand years ago, for example, in the time of Charlemagne? When our generation buries nuclear waste we do exactly that: we burden for centuries to come the generations that come after us with dangers that we, in furthering our own welfare, created. For it takes more than a thousand years for the life-threatening radiation of highly radioactive waste from nuclear power stations to subside. What sort of unforeseeable geological changes over the next thousand years, whether through earthquakes, floods or even meteor strikes, might be able to expose even the most secure of atomic waste containers?

The right to human dignity, the right to life and the right to personal development can exist only in a healthy environment. The right to a protected environment is a product of human dignity. If you do not respect Creation, you will ulti-mately trample human dignity. When children can no longer play outside because the ozone hole is too big, or when there is an increasing number of asthma attacks and incidents of cancer within the vicinity of a particular industrial plant, humanity's dignity is violated.

But how can this right to environmental protection be realised?

Can the parents of children whose health is endangered by ozone obtain, through the courts, restrictions on traffic? Can those who live on property that has been poisoned through prior use and whose health is threatened use the courts to demand new accommodation from the state or, at least, payment of compensation for suffering that they endure through no fault of their own? How can the next generation be defended from environmental damage that is caused by our generation, but which will have an effect only much later?

In the recent past, in many states, private associations and environmental protection organisations have acted as advocates of the environment. Their actions have led to judicial decisions that have awakened the consciousness of the public and caused politicians to make decisions in the interests of the environment. The right of associations to take legal action is an example of how legislatures can find new ways for the human right to environmental protection to be sensibly brought within the jurisdiction of the courts.

If you take human rights seriously you have to respect all dimensions of human development. Human dignity is only guaranteed when humans as beings endowed with Reason can develop in a social community and in a suitable environment. *Life that befits human dignity requires both freedom and an intact environment in which later generations can flourish.*

Many criticise this way of thinking because it puts humankind at the centre. As a matter of principle, it is said that not only human beings, but animals and plants, even the whole universe and Creation have rights that should be protected like human rights. "Advocates" of animals should thus receive the right to take legal action before the courts when measures such as animal experimentation would degrade animals.

Regardless of how environmental protection is understood, whether from the perspective of human beings or from the perspective of the dignity of the whole of Creation, in the end it will always be people in government buildings, parliaments or courts making decisions about what other people should do in the interests of the environment.

30
The Right to One's Own Language

Human beings without language are "dehumanised" creatures. The human can only make contact with other humans through language and symbols. Without language there is no communal social life. Because people can use language to communicate with other members of their species, the human is different from other life-forms. If you deprive people of speech, you rob them of their intrinsic identity. Now not all human beings speak the same language. Depending on their country, origin, tradition and educational standard every human speaks a language that cannot be understood by others. But everyone speaks the language that they spoke with their parents and their friends at school.

Language creates a sense of "us". The Swiss speak the Swiss-German language. Those who do not speak like the Swiss think differently, perhaps they even *are* different. People who want to integrate into Swiss society must first learn the language. By their accents they will however still be recognised as guests rather than as "real" Swiss.

The mother tongue is a part of the identity of every person. "I want my soul to go to heaven in Romansh", exclaimed a recent protagonist of the Romansh language, which is spoken in some Swiss cantons. Language is homeland. At present, many people can no longer use their own language, or can only use it in limited ways. In their country a different language is the language of the majority, and therefore the official language of social contact. Perhaps they emigrated with their parents to another country or perhaps their language is rejected, even suppressed, by the majority. Those who nevertheless want to stay in that country and to succeed must do so in a foreign language. This is difficult and requires lots of effort.

If you have to write to an official or fill in a form for the authorities, you want to be able to use your own language. You do not want to have to speak and write in a language of which you will never have full command.

Every language needs a culture. It has to be learned at school and extended through poets and intellectuals. But it also has to be refined and practised in daily use. A language which, like the national dress, is only taken out of the cupboard for festivals no longer has any living culture.

There is no doubt that the right to one's own language is an elementary human right. This human right is, however, much more difficult to secure than, for instance, the right to religious freedom. It is easy to imagine how people of very different religions can live next to and with each other. Religion is the intimate core of every single individual. It could be the same with language if everyone lived in isolation with only their own language. But we all know that that is not what happens. Language is never as private as religion. Indeed, it only consists and exists as a means of communication with other human beings. It only exists through the relevant community. That is why I can use my language. Even this is forbidden in some countries.

If I use a language only at the table with family and friends, but I am not allowed to use it in correspondence with the authorities, I am deeply dissatisfied. I pay my taxes and am entitled to expect that the authorities will speak with me in my tongue. But what is the position in areas in which people grow up speaking different languages? Can you demand of the authorities, of the postman, of the police, that they speak two or three languages, or even more? South Africa for instance recognises in its constitution eleven different national languages!

Furthermore, what is the position of the mass media? Do television and radio programs have to be broadcast in all languages? Who would finance the relevant programs? These difficulties mean that the human right to linguistic freedom cannot be treated like all the other individual rights.

Two almost irreconcilable principles oppose one another: the right to linguistic freedom on the one hand and the territorial principle on the other. In Belgium the territorial principle is applied almost without exception. According to this principle, in the respective linguistic region only one language is spoken, that is, the traditional majority language. Authorities that do not abide by this principle are punished. There is no linguistic freedom for speakers of other languages. This territorial principle is the collective linguistic right of the linguistic community.

In Switzerland this territorial principle is applied primarily to linguistic communities whose linguistic region is endangered, such as the regions of the Canton of Graubünden, in which the Romansh language is spoken. In comparison to both the large linguistic regions of French speaking and German speaking Switzerland, it remains controversial whether the territorial principle or the principle of linguistic freedom should be given priority in these regions.

The reason for these disagreements between the advocates of a collective right to a protected linguistic territory and those who want to further individual linguistic freedom as a human right, lies in the fact that both parties are convinced that they are protecting a human right. The individual linguistic right is expressed in general linguistic freedom. The territorial principle is an expression of a human right that can be developed only through and in the linguistic community. When the linguistic community no longer exists and the language is no longer spoken, linguistic freedom also is of no use. The human right to language can be realised only when both principles complement each other sensibly.

Nevertheless, in countries with linguistic groups that have been strongly mixed territorially in bi-lingual or multi-lingual cities such as Suva, in Fiji, or Brussels, in Belgium, it is not possible to protect minorities through the adoption of the territorial principle. Every linguistic community, therefore, has to have the opportunity to teach its own language, publish newspapers and even broadcast radio and television programs.

This linguistic federalism is tied to people. It is independent of territory, and accords linguistic communities certain rights to autonomy. It offers the only possible means for encouraging languages and cultures in mixed language regions.

There are presently very few states in which only a single language is spoken. Almost all states are confronted with the problem of linguistic freedom and the protection of minority languages. In almost all states linguistic minorities think that their state has not made sufficient provision for the human right to one's own language.

At the same time, advocates of the linguistic majority are almost always unanimous in their view that the public system has given the minority as much as the interests of the state and general welfare render possible; that any further step towards protecting the linguistic rights of the minority would lead to indirect discrimination against the linguistic majority.

Only those who are prepared to put themselves fully in the shoes of the linguistic minority will have sympathy for the demands that they make.

Ultimately the human right to language can only sensibly be realised when each society recognises that the cultural value of linguistic diversity is as important as that of the majority language. Recognition of this value ultimately must provide the basis for regulation of linguistic freedom and the territorial principle.

31

Ethnic Minorities within the State

The protection of ethnic minorities has become a theme of the utmost importance, particularly since the end of the great dispute between the communist and the Western capitalist states. For the world of the next century, publicists and political scientists predict countless conflicts between different cultures and peoples. We stand uncomprehending before large and bloody conflicts in the former Yugoslavia. We do not know how to react to the conflict in Chechnya. We repress knowledge of the massacres on the African and the Asiatic continents about which we hear daily. In doing so we forget all too quickly that even Western Europe has only managed these issues in a very limited way.

Can the problems of minorities be solved through an improvement of human rights? In states that are only just being formed, it is next to impossible to solve the problem of protecting minorities through traditional human rights mechanisms. For, in these circumstances, the state means everything to the nation which the majority represents and nothing to the minorities within it. These minorities end up virtually without rights or have to issue declarations of loyalty to the majority, declarations which they perceive to be degrading. If they do not do so they lose their citizenship. Citizenship in turn gives an entitlement to property, housing and business as well as to work and social benefits. Thus people who belonged to the original population become foreign workers in their own state. In many cases they are at the mercy of the police. They are ostracised from a majority society that labels them parasites.

The present centrality of the issues of minorities is not only a challenge for human rights, but also to the state as such. Minorities do not want a state that was created by a majority hostile towards them and that did not even seek their approval. And from the standpoint of human rights clearly it is fundamental that the minority is also loyal, and that the state and the authorities, which are supposed to protect the minority, are accepted as a matter of principle.

A number of years ago a delegation from the "Conference on Security and Cooperation in Europe" recommended to the then self-proclaimed Parliament of Kosovo that in order to protect minorities particular observers from the CSCE be sent as ombudsmen. This was rejected by some advocates of the Albanian minority on the grounds that such observers would have had to work together with the Serbian authorities and thus only contribute to the legitimacy of the Serbian state. This was of absolutely no value to the minority in Kosovo. They did not want to live under Serbian sovereignty any longer, nor support the protection of Serbian human rights. They wanted instead to create their own state.

This claim shows the drama of the present problem of minority protection in a multicultural state. In many regions, minority protection is seen to involve more than human rights. Minority protection is supposed to give the minorities the opportunity to create their own state.

Traditionally, in the practice of many states, a majority has almost unrestricted power. Judicial authorities can intervene only in restricted cases. On the European continent, at least, they tend not to have the jurisdiction which the courts of the United States possess. When the majority sets itself the goal, as is sadly the case in many states, of misusing the state for its own national and cultural interests, and thereby suppressing the minority, the minority is defenceless. The majority and the state which serves the majority lose all credibility. The minority will do everything to create its own state or to emigrate from that state.

This might be avoided if the minority, like everyone else, is able to participate in a multicultural state that is established in a way which ensures that the minority will not be outvoted by use of the principle of majority rule. In other words, if a state is founded on a consensus of the majority and the minority, members of the minority can identify with the state just like members of the majority.

But this means that the traditional democratic principle of majority rule does not provide an adequate solution to minority questions. New procedures and institutions are required to take the position of the minority into account. *The minorities problem is a challenge to the basis of the state, but also to human rights themselves.*

Solutions that lead to a total separation of minorities from the mother state are as unappealing as total oppression. The example of Yugoslavia demonstrated this clearly. People wanted to solve minorities problems through recognition of new republics. This created minority problems that were even more severe and insoluble. For every ethnic group which demanded self-determination and the creation of a new state on its territory, found itself confronted with a new minority. These minorities were even more reluctant to accept the new state if they used to be a majority.

Such members of the majority, like the Serbs in Yugoslavia or the Unionists in Northern Ireland, use all available means to fight against secession. They fear that, if they are severed from their mother state, they will experience the same minority fate as that experienced by the minority currently seeking self-determination. They will therefore fight using all available means for the retention of the status quo. They may be able to convince the majority to use state-sanctioned terror in order to suppress excessive aspirations for autonomy by the minority.

If one accuses these state authorities of terrorising the minority and suppressing them through increasingly grave violations of human rights, they will reply: "How can you on the one hand demand the protection of human rights by state authorities, while on the other hand you deny the state any form of legitimacy?"

Many of these states also claim that, ultimately, their right to statehood is a human right that must be observed by the international community. Turkey, for instance, in adopting the ideals of the French Revolution, developed into a secular state based on freedom, democracy and sovereignty. When state unity is questioned, the whole basis of the Turkish state is undermined. So citizens who raise the Kurdish question are treated as enemies of the state, just as much as those in Western democracies who combat the state as such.

The Kurds as well as many other minorities claim their collective human rights. They demand that their right to their own culture and language and to autonomy be recognised as a human right. People are not isolated beings whose rights come only through their individuality. They are embedded in communities that have developed over time, been shaped by religion and held together through language. Indisputably, these roots are part of everyone's identity. If you deny collective rights to groups and communities, you ultimately deny that individuals are part of these communities.

Opponents of collective rights counter that such rights ultimately undermine the freedom of the individual. If you preserve the collective right of the community, how can individuals who do not identify with the relevant community exist and survive? Will the collective right of the community not also give it the right and the authority to use force in the interests of the community's culture to thwart all individuality, and hence also individual human rights?

Here we have two opposing points of view without a bridge between them. There is no easy compromise, beyond the need to recognise the value of the lone individual and the value of community itself without which the individual could not exist. Where the line is to be drawn in particular cases is a question that can only be solved gradually and pragmatically in the light of experience.

Majorities and minorities have to be ready to reconsider the foundations of their states once again. If they are not prepared to rebuild the state anew, so that it becomes a homeland for both majorities and minorities, no solution will be found. But this requires a new understanding of the state that not only recognises an atomised society of lone individuals with equal rights, but also acknowledges that communities must voluntarily be included in the greater state society.

So long as people stick to the view that state sovereignty is unrestricted and gives the majority the right to rule without the democratic consensus of the minority, majorities and minorities will fight over this sovereignty relentlessly and a solution to the conflict will remain unforeseeable.

32

Human Rights in War

It is often claimed that war is itself a violation of human rights. And yet many of the pioneers of human rights, including Henri Dunant, the founder of the Red Cross, and others, tried desperately to help at least the victims of war. The many international conventions for the protection of war victims were the early attempts to use international treaties to protect human rights during times of war.

Through these conventions one can try to help non-combatants, such as the civilian population, the sick and wounded, and even prisoners, who, being defenceless, are at the mercy of warring soldiers. In order to help these people during times of war the International Committee of the Red Cross is supposed to be neutral as between all the warring parties, in order to look after the defenceless.

But the face of war has changed fundamentally since the foundation of the Red Cross. Previously princes fought over countries and peoples which they wanted to conquer. Then nations fought over ideologies. Communists wanted to re-educate entire ethnic communities and commit them to their ideology. In these circumstances it was next to impossible to protect human rights. The goal of a war was to change people, to re-educate them, to "force them into freedom".

Wars of liberation against colonialist states were waged by small groups of rebels who used human rights violations as weapons of terror. It was only when they reduced people to fear that they succeeded, or so they thought, in bringing on the fall of the hated regime of the colonialist state. In these cases the only solution may be later to make those responsible for terror campaigns accountable before an international tribunal.

In most wars in today's world ethnic groups fight over territory. They do not want to exterminate opposing ethnic groups. They just want to expel them from "their territory". In order to achieve this goal, the warring parties will shrink from no atrocity: all parties in such wars humiliate ethnic groups through systematic rape, the brutal expulsion of people from their own homes, massacres and intimidation through atrocious forms of torture and terror.

But how do people let themselves be drawn into such civil wars? How can a normal citizen from one day to the next become a sniper, torturer or terrorist? People will be quick to sign-up as volunteers to save their own ethnic group and their families if they think that the opposition will be an enemy who will shrink from no atrocity, who will rape and torture women and children. They will hardly reproach themselves when they shoot enemies in an ambush if those enemies have been demonised by media and propaganda.

Thus information about the most atrocious violations of human rights, mixed with propaganda, half truths and exaggerations, itself becomes a cause and justification for further actions of the most brutal sort.

Who can provide effective support for human rights in such cases? Human rights are no instruments of international politics. *If you really want to support human rights you do not as a first priority denounce the warring parties, you instead look primarily to the welfare of the victims.* You try to help the victims, regardless of race, religion or ethnic nationality. By contrast, those who let themselves use violations of human rights as a tool of war will only contribute to greater suffering and even more devastating violations of human rights.

War crimes are the most brutal violations of human rights. They must be criminalised and punished universally, that is, all over the entire world, regardless of whether they are perpetrated by the criminals of a great power or committed by the thugs of a state that has been excluded from the international community.

But the idea of human rights does not require entire ethnic groups to be condemned for the acts of individuals. The demonisation of an ethnic group violates the elementary human rights of individual members of the group, members who are in no way to blame for the atrocities of their countrymen. After World War Two the Allies in occupied Germany prohibited their own soldiers from speaking to German children! It is a basic cornerstone of all human rights that for each atrocity only those who actually committed it are allowed to be made responsible. Collective punishment and the liability of all members of a family for the crimes of one member are not only violations of the human dignity of individual people: they are also the cause of new wars and campaigns of revenge by ethnic groups, races, tribes and states.

33

Auschwitz

Anyone who has ever visited the former Auschwitz concentration camp will remember the images forever: mountains of small children's cases with puppets and toys lie carefully piled high in large rooms, as if they are waiting to be finally collected by their small owners. On many of the little cases one can still read the lovingly chalked names of Rebekka, Esther, Isaak and other names of millions of innocent children and their families, whom the thugs herded into the gas chambers.

Auschwitz is the most appalling incident recorded in the history of humanity. Until the decision of Hitler's national socialist Germany on the "Final Solution", a state had never passed laws for the total elimination of a defenceless ethnic group. Ethnic groups had been enslaved and conquered, ethnic groups had been and still are driven from their land. Never in history had a state had the inhumanity and the arrogance to declare an ethnic group, which had never endangered it, to be utterly worthless and to attempt to totally destroy them. The consequences of these laws were the most appalling human rights violations that the history of humanity has yet seen.

How was such a thing possible? Could it happen again? Such questions are raised anxiously by many people. Indeed, the most appalling human rights violations of all time did not become reality over night; they were a result of age-old discrimination and hate campaigns against the Jewish people. Many Christians have always held Jewish people as a whole responsible for the death of Jesus. This hate has, over the centuries, led to pogroms against the Jews again and again. Yet today there are noted legal historians who prove that the trial of Jesus could not have been run in accordance with old Jewish law as it is described in the Bible, and that therefore even the Jews from that period cannot be held responsible for the death of Jesus.

It is never permissible for a person to be burdened with guilt for conduct for which they were not responsible. But how often do we all fall into the trap of generalising about people that are different? A group of foreigners commit a crime; so all members of that ethnic group are labelled as constituting a public danger.

If you give superior status to particular people ethnically, culturally, spiritually or intellectually, you denigrate at the same time all those who have not been able to drink from the fountain of that culture, that ethnic group, that religion, that race. These "inferior human beings" have fewer or even no rights, and if they get in the way of the "superior human beings" in their drive to freedom they are perceived as merely useless vermin who have to be exterminated. National Socialism converted the most terrifying consequences of racist thought into action.

But how was it possible that individual human beings like you and I were prepared to torture innocent people, slaughter babies, conduct the most appalling and painful of experiments on children, select people for the gas chambers and even, as commandants of camps, shoot down, just for fun, individual camp inmates who, while on the way to work, happened to catch their eye.

Such atrocities really can never be fully explained. Many people who commit such acts justify themselves by claiming that their victims were not even human, were mere rats, vermin that had to be exterminated. They thus lead us back to the real masterminds behind the scenes who wanted to prove that there are different classes of people that should be treated differently according to race, religion, ethnic and linguistic membership. Someone who does not recognise that people as a matter of principle have equal rights and are of equal value, someone who circulates such "Non-Teachings" through the media and other forms of propaganda, someone who in addition fans the flames of hate against other ethnic groups, someone who spreads fear. These people share the responsibility for the thugs who led people to the gas chambers.

But the countless people who are indifferent, who are not prepared to stand up for human dignity and human rights, are also jointly responsible. The indifferent protested neither domestically nor from abroad when, as early as 1935, the Nuremberg Laws, which were known to the public, prescribed the most appalling discrimination and humiliation of the Jewish people. The indifferent mounted no resistance when Swiss diplomats and representatives of Germany agreed to introduce the Jewish stamp in the passports of German Jews, which the Swiss authorities used to prevent German Jews from fleeing to Switzerland. When in the 1930s Italy's fascist regime demanded that professors take an oath to fascism in which they would swear to educate students to be loyal members of fascist Italy, only about 0.5% of the 3000 professors refused to take the oath. The Catholic Church, for instance, with the dubious excuse that fascism was to be equated with the Italian State, deluded itself and thus justified its signing of the document. The indifferent, who are worried only about their own well-being, are the surface on which the carpet is rolled out for dictators and inciters of ethnic hatred.

Radical leaders of parties usually have an easy time winning the indifferent over to their cause. With hate propaganda and promises the indifferent can be won for the first small atrocity. Those who let themselves be integrated into the circle of criminals search for justifications in order to cleanse their conscience from the stain of atrocities. These justifications can be found in tracts which reduce entire races, religions and ethnic groups to second class human beings, declaring them to be hated enemies, while also extolling one ethnic group as a morally superior group of rulers.

34

Human Rights on Either Side of the Atlantic

In New York the cost of using public transport has gone up. Those affected are first and foremost the various ethnic minorities who live in the outer suburbs and are reliant on public transport. The minorities know that neither a strike nor a public protest in the "colour-blind" consumer society will improve their situation. That is why they are trying to use the courts to force the public transport administrators to stabilise prices, because, so they argue, the increase in prices is an outrageous violation of equal rights.

By contrast, in Europe, the situation is different. For example, the Germans of Danish origin in Schleswig-Holstein could not take legal action against price increases on the German railway, even if it disadvantaged them in travelling to Hamburg, as compared to other Germans. And the Genevans were not able to force the Swiss Government, through the courts, to expand their airport, making it comparable to the airfield in Zürich, so that the French speaking minority in Geneva was not disadvantaged.

In Paris the police hit out at demonstrating students. An American observer wonders why those affected do not take action in the courts, so that the police are disciplined and made to treat demonstrators respectfully. The American does not know that while American courts can grant a remedy in such situations, the European courts cannot. Someone who wants to force the administration to behave properly cannot do so through a court in Europe, because courts are not allowed to deal with such actions.

In Boston Massachusetts the management of a school stubbornly refuses to admit minorities to the school. Without further ado, a court decides to place the school under the management of a fellow judge, from now on. Such a decision is unthinkable for a European court. It would not have the power to do such a thing. Nor would a judge ever think of taking the enforcement of the law into her own hands, even if the administration obstinately refused to observe certain human rights. In Europe, courts generally can only overturn administrative decisions. They cannot make their own administrative decisions, nor order particular measures against the administration.

At the annual congress of the American Rifle Association (a lobby group for the owners of weapons) the Association's president declared that the right of every citizens to own his own weapon was not only guaranteed in the American Bill of Rights, but it was a *God given right*, that could be restricted by neither the state nor the constitution.

These examples show how differently human rights and the role of the courts in relation to them are perceived in the United States and Europe respectively. Why have such differing legal interpretations of the position and task of the judge in the enforcement of human rights developed in these two continents?

France and the United States see themselves today as the real pioneers of human rights. In France it was the revolutionary National Assembly of the Three Estates which, in

August 1789, forced the human rights declaration from King Louis XVI. The people received from the hands of their representatives, as the first gift of the Revolution, the Declaration of the Rights of Man, in those days still signed by the King.

Then Napoleon, as a liberal dictator, created a state for himself, with a view to converting an aristocratic society into a liberal one. He saw the state as an instrument with which he could do this. But so that the state could achieve his goals, it had to have strong leadership. Above all, it could not be exposed to the review of conservative judges. That is why he created a new type of law, so called "public law", which from then on was applied to the administration of the state. As the administration alone was bound by this public law, citizens could not get any protection against arbitrary regulations before normal courts. It was only through the tedious and lengthy work of the legislature that politicians were in a position, through the introduction of administrative courts and constitutional courts, to once again subject the administration – at least to some degree – to judicial review.

For many Americans, a state is a collective that suppresses individual freedom. The state as a unit is foreign to American legal thinking. There cannot be state goals such as the protection of freedom. In the United States you talk of government instead of the state. In doing so, you refer to all the higher institutions of state, to which the legislature, the president and the judges belong, but not to one "state" which encompasses the whole collective. It is not the task of the government, that is, the institutions of government, to change society. Instead, the government is supposed to balance the various opposing social forces and mediate between them. The legislature mediates through new laws, the president through executive measures and the judiciary as the third branch through corrective judicial decisions.

In common law countries, such as the United States, the state is not an instrument that can be used to change society. That is why, for Americans, the European continental division of law into private law and public law is so foreign. In America, human rights are still the preserve of traditional courts. If a case arises, they can decide between the legislature and the executive in the same way as between one private citizen and another.

The understanding of human rights is hence totally different in the United States. Neither the state nor the founding fathers of the Constitution gave human beings their human rights. On their understanding these rights stand above the Constitution. They are God given inalienable natural rights. So on either side of the Atlantic a fundamentally different understanding of rights and courts in general, and human rights in particular, has developed.

In the United States human rights are administered and protected in practice solely through the courts. They exist independently of statute, even of the Constitution. They are part of the "rule of law". The courts and judges are supposed to ensure that the people are ruled not by people, but through law. Human rights cannot, as with the European interpretation, be protected through the Constitution and then withdrawn once more. They are not the plaything of politics. They are embedded in the idea of justice, which can only be entrusted to the third branch, that is, to the courts.

According to the European understanding, the rights of citizens were first created through the constitution and statute. It is the task of the judge to interpret the rights given to citizens in the constitution and statute, in order to ascertain whether their complaints are valid. The law has to ensure that those who are in the right receive justice before the judge. Judge and court are in the service of the rights entrenched in the constitution and statute.

In the United States people have inalienable rights which the legislature can neither give nor take away from them. Everything which by nature belongs to Man is inalienable and must be protected, just like property in worldly goods, according to James Madison, the most important founding father. What humans think, what they say and write, their religion, their occupation, the moral values to which they are attached, the freedom of their person, these are all part of their property. If it is damaged, a person affected must be able to go to a judge and demand compensation for the deprivation of intellectual, emotional and material values.

Judges for their part, do not see themselves as serving the political majority who enacted the country's statutes. They see themselves as serving justice, that is, the "rule of law". A judge must make a reasonable ruling on a conflict between two parties (eg the police and a citizen) who are seeking their rights. In the actual dispute, a party will only be in the right once it has won the case. For the judge creates new law, and does not merely interpret existing laws. To ensure that a judgment is just, a judge must give both parties a fair chance to win the case. A judge must treat the parties fairly. This is, therefore, necessarily, the most important human right.

Compare a legal dispute before a judge with a game of chess. In the United States the human right can be compared with an additional queen, with which the position of the party who can invoke the human right is substantially improved. If you can invoke your human rights, you will be able substantially to improve your long-term social and societal position through the courts.

In Europe, human rights and the courts are largely in the service of the majority. But in the United States judges, with the help of human rights, can protect minorities from the majority. They did this particularly in the 1960s and 1970s. The decisions of the Supreme Court over the past few years, however, suggest a fundamental change in the dispensation of justice. Many observers now seriously doubt whether the courts are still willing and prepared to use their authority to protect ethnic minorities from the increasing power of the majority. For the majority, the "American mainstream", has discovered anew the human right to freedom of trade and contract. And with this "exchange of pawns", judges, impressed by the value of achievement, are supposed to be forced once more, in the interests of welfare optimisation, to make decisions that are "colour-", "race-" and "culture-blind", based solely on the basis of achievement and not on the basis of membership of some sort of ethnic community.

35

Summary

The biggest dangers for human rights lurk with those who rule, who boast about such rights and misuse them for their election propaganda. A member of a government who takes human rights seriously will concede willingly that they make governing difficult. Yet she will also subject herself to the burden of human rights. She recognises that, through esteem and respect for the human dignity of each individual, a much higher good can be won: confidence in state and government.

   Human rights are effectively protected only when there is a separation between the institutions of a state and reciprocal checks and balances, so that people who serve in these institutions, whether as heads of state, members of the government, legislature or judiciary, must take human rights seriously in their daily work.

   As uncontroversial as the principle of human rights is, it is difficult to secure human rights in specific cases. The line between the freedom of the individual, which is to be protected as against the community, and the rights of the community as against sole individuals, will in concrete cases always need to be drawn anew.

   Anyone who entrusts human rights to the protection of political authorities is naive. Ultimately, only independent courts and ombudsmen equipped with the relevant authority can guarantee that parliaments, governments and administrations will not misuse their power. They are in the best position to ensure in a way that is credible, that human rights serve the weak and the defenceless, rather than merely the powerful. Human rights are only protected in a state which rules through law and not through people.

If the acts of government in the area of human rights cannot be examined nor reviewed, those who govern invariably will let their own administration and police talk them into believing that, in a specific case, the superior interests of the state make it necessary to restrict freedom and human rights. With references to "reasons of state" such acts can always be justified to the public; in the interests of the welfare of the state such arguments always appear, superficially, tenable. Political parties are hardly concerned with the question of whether the price, that is, the violation of human rights, is too high in a specific case. Only courts and ombudsmen have to take each specific case seriously.

If all human beings were angels we would not need human rights. Human rights are necessary because we know from experience that human beings must not be entrusted with unchecked power. All human beings who can exercise unchecked power are vulnerable to the temptation to give in to their aggressions, to satisfy their frustrations and let the defenceless, who are under their control, feel their power. And, if they think of people within their control as real or potential rivals, or as members of an inferior group, reservations which might otherwise make them shrink from intimidation, exploitation or even torture and rape, quickly evaporate.

If all human beings were devils, every discussion of human rights would be equally futile. For then even the best institutions would be able to do nothing to make those who govern, and members of the administration, respect human rights and devote their energies solely to their real responsibilities. Precisely because human beings are neither angels nor devils we are entitled to expect that those who govern, and officials who have power over the defenceless, will learn from supervision, criticism and bad experiences. We are entitled to count on them to take all necessary steps to avoid criticism from independent review bodies, and to abide by the guidelines and instructions of superior authorities. If government and officials are subject to review by other institutions this will curb any tendency to display and accumulate power.

In states with ethnic minorities that cannot stand up to the democratic majority there is a danger of human rights violations if the majority controls everything and makes all the decisions. To justify its supremacy the majority may support those parts of the media which fan the hate of one community against another, the minority community. Thus a climate of violence and resentment develops in which the protection of human rights is hopeless.

Poverty and the social decline of a society also are serious dangers for the protection of human rights. They undermine the credibility of the state and the legal order amongst the unemployed and the marginalised. These, in turn, either vent their aggression in their own way or, in frustration, take revenge on the society's defenceless foreigners. If the state gradually dissolves into a powerless organisation, tears itself apart and falls under the wheel of corruption and crime, it will always be the weak who pay dearly for it first.

Human rights unfortunately are all too often a weapon that is ineffective against the powerful in the state and society. Human rights ultimately have a chance only in states in which law is observed and enforced. A state in which the law can no longer protect will no longer be able to guarantee human rights.

In the philosophy of Confucius, now more that 2000 years old, there is a saying which both states, and the international community, should take to heart, just like the princes of old:

The disciple asked his Master: "What does a state need when it wants to give people peace and justice?" The Master replied: "It needs a good army, sufficient food and the confidence of the people." The disciple was not satisfied with the answer: "But of these three, which is the easiest to do without, when the state cannot have all three?", asked he who thirsts for knowledge of his teacher. "The army", was the answer. "Yes, and which could the state then do without, if it could only have one of these three? What is absolutely necessary for a state to exist and for the government to govern?" the disciple still wanted to know. "Confidence. Without confidence there is neither a state nor a government", the Master answered him.

We find the basis for this confidence in constitutions and in state institutions which must ensure that governments take the protection of human rights seriously.

The Universal Declaration of Human Rights

Preamble

Whereas recognition of the inherent dignity and of the equal and inalienable rights of all members of the human family is the foundation of freedom, justice and peace in the world,

Whereas disregard and contempt for human rights have resulted in barbarous acts which have outraged the conscience of Mankind, and the advent of a world in which human beings shall enjoy freedom and belief and freedom from fear and want has been proclaimed as the highest aspiration of the common people,

Whereas, it is essential, if Man is not to be compelled to have recourse, as a last resort, to rebellion against tyranny and oppression, that human rights should be protected by the rule of law,

Whereas it is essential to promote the development of friendly relations between nations,

Whereas the peoples of the United Nations have in the Charter reaffirmed their faith in fundamental human rights, in the dignity and worth of the human person and in the equal rights of men and women and have determined to promote social progress and better standards of life in larger freedom,

Whereas member states have pledged themselves to achieve, in cooperation with the United Nations, the promotion of universal respect for and observance of human rights and fundamental freedoms,

Whereas a common understanding of these rights and freedoms is of the greatest importance for the full realisation of this pledge,

Now, therefore, The General Assembly, Proclaims this Universal Declaration of Human Rights as a common standard of achievement for all peoples and all nations, to the end that every individual and every organ of society, keeping this Declaration constantly in mind, shall strive by teaching and education to promote respect for these rights and freedoms and by progressive measures, national and international, to secure their universal and effective recognition and observance, both among the peoples of member states themselves and among the peoples of territories under their jurisdiction.

Article 1

All human beings are born free and equal in dignity and rights. They are endowed with reason and conscience and should act towards one another in a spirit of brotherhood.

Article 2

Everyone is entitled to all the rights and freedoms set forth in this Declaration, without distinction of any kind, such as race, colour, sex, language, religion, political or other opinion, national or social origin, property, birth or other status. Furthermore, no distinction shall be made on the basis of political, jurisdictional or international status of the country or territory to which a person belongs, whether it be independent, trust, non-self-governing or under any other limitation of sovereignty.

Article 3

Everyone has the right to life, liberty and security of person.

Article 4

No-one shall be held in slavery or servitude; slavery and the slave trade shall be prohibited in all their forms.

Article 5

No-one shall be subjected to torture or to cruel, inhuman or degrading treatment and punishment.

Article 6

Everyone has the right to recognition everywhere as a person before the law.

Article 7

All are equal before the law and are entitled without any discrimination to equal protection of the law. All are entitled to equal protection against any discrimination in violation of this Declaration and against any incitement to such discrimination.

Article 8

Everyone has the right to an effective remedy by the competent national tribunals for acts violating the fundamental rights granted him by the constitution or by law.

Article 9

No-one shall be subjected to arbitrary arrest, detention or exile.

Article 10

Everyone is entitled in full equality to a fair and public hearing by an independent and impartial tribunal, in the determination of his rights and obligations and of any criminal charge against him.

Article 11

1. Everyone charged with a penal offence has the right to be presumed innocent until proven guilty according to law in a public trial at which he has had all the guarantees necessary for his defence.

2. No-one shall be held guilty of any penal offence on account of any act or omission which did not constitute a penal offence, under national or international law, at the time when it was committed. Nor shall a heavier penalty be imposed than the one that was applicable at the time the penal offence was committed.

Article 12

No-one shall be subjected to arbitrary interference with his privacy, family, home or correspondence, not to attacks upon his honour and reputation. Everyone has the right to the protection of the law against such interference or attacks.

Article 13

1. Everyone has the right to freedom of movement and residence within the borders of each state.

2. Everyone has the right to leave any country, including his own, and to return to his country.

Article 14

1. Everyone has the right to seek and to enjoy in other countries asylum from persecution.

2. This right may not be invoked in the case of prosecutions genuinely arising from non-political crimes or from acts contrary to the purposes and principles of the United Nations.

Article 15

1. Everyone has the right to a nationality.
2. No-one shall be arbitrarily deprived of his nationality nor denied the right to change his nationality.

Article 16

1. Men and women of full age, without limitation due to race, nationality or religion, have the right to marry and found a family. They are entitled to equal rights to marriage, during marriage and at its dissolution.
2. Marriage shall be entered into only with the free and full consent of the intending spouses.
3. The family is the natural and fundamental group unit of society and is entitled to protection by society and the State.

Article 17

1. Everyone has the right to own property alone as well as in association with others.
2. No-one shall be arbitrarily deprived of his property.

Article 18

Everyone has the right to freedom of thought, conscience and religion; this right includes freedom to change his religion or belief, and freedom, either alone or in community with others and in public or private, to manifest his religion or belief in teaching, practice, worship and observance.

Article 19

Everyone has the right to freedom of opinion and expression; this right includes freedom to hold opinions without interference and to seek, receive and impart information and ideas through any media and regardless of frontiers.

Article 20

1. Everyone has the right to freedom of peaceful assembly and association.

2. No-one may be compelled to belong to an association.

Article 21

1. Everyone has the right to take part in the government of his country, directly or through freely chosen representatives.

2. Everyone has the right of equal access to public services in his country.

3. The will of the people shall be the basis of the authority of government; this will shall be expressed in periodic and genuine elections which shall be by universal and equal suffrage and shall be held by secret vote or by equivalent free voting procedures.

Article 22

Everyone, as a member of society, has the right to social security and is entitled to realisation through national effort and international cooperation and in accordance with the organisation and resources of each State, of the economic, social and cultural rights indispensable for his dignity and the free development of character.

Article 23

1. Everyone has the right to work, to free choice of employment, to just and favourable conditions of work and to protection against unemployment.

2. Everyone, without any discrimination, has the right to equal pay for equal work.

3. Everyone who works has the right to just and favourable remuneration ensuring for himself and his family an existence worthy of human dignity, and supplemented, if necessary, by other means of social protection.

4. Everyone has the right to form and to join trade unions for the protection of his interests.

Article 24

Everyone has the right to rest and leisure, including reasonable limitation of working hours and period holidays with pay.

Article 25

1. Everyone has the right to a standard of living adequate for the health and well-being of himself and his family, including food, clothing, housing and medical care and necessary social services, and the right to security in the event of unemployment, sickness, disability, widowhood, old age or other lack of livelihood in circumstances beyond his control.

2. Motherhood and childhood are entitled to special care and assistance. All children, whether born in or out of wedlock, shall enjoy the same protection.

Article 26

1. Everyone has the right to education. Education shall be free, at least in the elementary and fundamental stages. Elementary education shall be compulsory. Technical and professional education shall be made generally available and higher education shall be equally accessible to all on the basis of merit.

2. Education shall be directed to the full development of the human personality and the strengthening of respect for human rights and fundamental freedoms. It shall promote understanding, tolerance and friendship among all nations, racial or religious groups, and shall further the activities of the United Nations for the maintenance of peace.

3. Parents have a prior right to choose the kind of education that shall be given to their children.

Article 27

1. Everyone has the right to participate in the cultural life of the community, to enjoy the arts and to share in scientific advancement and its benefits.

2. Everyone has the right to protection of the moral and material interests resulting from any scientific, literary or artistic production of which he is the author.

Article 28

Everyone is entitled to a social and international order in which the rights and freedoms set forth in the Declaration can be fully realised.

Article 29

1. Everyone has the duties to the community in which alone the free and full development of his personality is possible.

2. In the exercise of his rights and freedoms, everyone shall be subject only to such limitations as are determined by law solely for the purpose of securing due recognition and respect for the rights and freedoms of others and of meeting the just requirements of morality, public order and the general welfare in a democratic society.

3. These rights and freedoms may in no case be exercised
    contrary to the purposes and principles of the United
    Nations.

Article 30

Nothing in this Declaration may be interpreted as implying for
any State, group or person any right to engage in any activity or
to perform any act aimed at the destruction of any the rights
and freedoms set forth herein.

Index

Africa
human rights abuses in, 4

Asylum
deportation of asylum seekers without trial, 23
prohibition on deportation of asylum seekers to a country where well-founded fear of torture, 23
relationship to human dignity, 67
right to asylum not a recognised human right, 21

Auschwitz, 129

Australia
denial of indigenous Australians' right to vote under Constitution and legislation, 79
publication of article on shoplifting by student newspaper, 101
surveillance of suspected communists, 87
use of commission to invest police misconduct in Queensland, 28

Balkans
political use of human and minority rights in, 5

Baltic countries
oppression of the Russian minority in, 5

Cambodia
calls for human rights to be observed and monitored in, 4

China
calls for human rights to be observed in, 4
rejection of human rights as political tools by, 6

Conflicts between and limits on human rights
ability of courts to balance human rights, social harmony and needs of the public purse, 106
conflicts between civil and political rights and social rights, 106
proportionality, 59
public interest, 80
resolution by legislature rather than executive, 58, 77

Democracy and human rights
citizen's veto of laws in Switzerland, 78
democracy and self-determination, 40
relationship between, 38

Human nature
   as divided into two classes, 130-1
   design of institutions and, 44-5
   Enlightenment view of, 16
   Hobbes on, 33, 43
   human beings as endowed with Reason, 1, 16, 37
   Lord Acton on, 44
   Marxist view of, 17
   nationalism and, 17
   Nazi interpretation of, 17, 130-1
   relationship between Enlightenment view of human nature and popular sovereignty, 37
   relationship between human rights and human Reason, 16
   relationship with freedom of the press, 103-4

Human rights and property
   distribution of property, 69-70
   relationship with right to work, 70
   right to hold private property, 70
   use of private property, 70

Human rights and the police, 51-55
   Amnesty International, 84
   arbitrary search and seizure, 82-3
   incommunicados, 83
   International Committee of the Red Cross, 83-4
   obligation to inform accused of their rights, 62
   police powers of detention in Anglo-Saxon and European countries, 52-4, 60-1
   protection of human rights by police, 85
   right to habeas corpus, 60-1
   right to habeas corpus and judicial independence, 62
   tension between protection of population from violent crime and rights of accused, 62-3
   under state of emergency, 63

Human rights in employment, 9

Human rights instruments
   American Declaration of Independence, 15
   Bill of Rights of the Constitution of the United States, 15
   Bill of Rights, 15
   Declaration of the Rights of Man, 15
   European Convention for the Protection of Human Rights and Fundamental Freedoms, 5
   role of, 35-6
   Universal Declaration of Human Rights, 73, 143

Minorities (*cont*)
role of courts in protecting rights of, 21, 75, 80,
separatism by minorities in Eastern Europe, 39

Montesquieu
checks and balances, 27
justification for the separation of powers, 27

Ombudsmen, 89-90, 139

Politicisation of human rights, 5, 85, 127-8.

Right of revolution, 15

Right to a fair trial, 60
Belilos Case before European Court of Human Rights, 20, 21
common law and civil law trials compared, 48-9
need for impartiality, independence and careful investigation, 50
need for legal certainty, 83

Right to appoint a government, 15

Right to bear arms, 134

Right to life
abortion and, 80
death penalty and, 6
relationship with an intact environment, 114

Right to physical integrity
absolute right to, 31
human dignity and, 2-3
monopoly on force, 11, 91, 92
use of torture in criminal investigations and, 48

Right to privacy, 87
protection through ombudsmen, 89

Right to self-determination, 40-41

Right to unimpeded personal development
levels of income and, 9
restrictions on, 8, 93
smoking and, 91-3

Right to vote and stand for office
foreigners and, 96

Rights in criminal proceedings, 48-9
death penalty, 6, 63-4